D0886166

Technology and the School Library

A Comprehensive Guide for Media Specialists and Other Educators

Revised Edition

Odin L. Jurkowski

THE SCARECROW PRESS, INC.
Lanham • Toronto • Plymouth, UK

Published by Scarecrow Press, Inc.
A wholly owned subsidiary of The Rowman & Littlefield Publishing Group, Inc.
4501 Forbes Boulevard, Suite 200, Lanham, Maryland 20706
http://www.scarecrowpress.com

Estover Road, Plymouth PL6 7PY, United Kingdom

British Library Cataloguing in Publication Information Available

Library of Congress Cataloging-in-Publication Data

Jurkowski, Odin L., 1969–
  Technology and the school library : a comprehensive guide for media
specialists and other educators / Odin L. Jurkowski. — Rev. ed.
      p. cm.
  Includes bibliographical references and index.
  ISBN 978-0-8108-7448-0 (pbk. : alk. paper) — ISBN 978-0-8108-7449-7
(ebook)
  1. School libraries—Information technology. 2. School libraries—
Automation. 3. Instructional materials centers—Information technology.
4. Instructional materials centers—Automation. 5. Internet in school
libraries. 6. Educational technology. I. Title.
  Z675.S3J87 2010
  027.8—dc22
                                                        2010000155

Printed in the United States of America

Contents

Introduction

No individual school contains all the resources and information that students need to master to flourish in the twenty-first century.[1]

The school library has evolved with a degree of complexity that mirrors changes throughout education, our local communities, and society at large. Once viewed as merely a storehouse of printed books with a zealous librarian advocating reading literacy, libraries have changed with technological advances that allow us to provide more resources in a dizzying array of formats and access to information from outside library walls. This isn't to say that we don't still have energetic librarians who love reading and promoting books, but now there's more. We can reach out to the classrooms, and our students can interact with the world. Parallel to these changes, school librarians must evolve as well. There's a never-ending need for lifelong learning and continuing education in order to keep pace. We're all too familiar with the excitement of buying a new piece of technology only to find out the next week that there's something newer, faster, smaller, and better—and, of course, at a much lower price.

Although funding is always an issue, education in general has embraced technology. Technology has been viewed as a way to increase student motivation, to provide resources, to make instruction easier and more effective, and to improve student learning. Although marked results and studies verify these beliefs,[2] some visionary ideas have never come to pass, and we look back on them with improved hindsight. For example, when the phonograph was invented, educators looked to a future where students would listen to prerecorded lessons instead of having to listen to a teacher lecture, thereby allowing schools to cut back on "costly" personnel. Similar ideas came about later with the development of television; some educators pictured students simply watching programs produced by a select few expert teachers. In this case, visual learning in combination with the older aural was seen as an improvement that would revolutionize education. Similar cost-saving beliefs crop up with each new technology, with people claiming that the latest developments have finally reached a potential for productivity gains and lower costs. Each time, these beliefs are rebuffed. We're now just beginning to realize that the direct interaction of the teacher and librarian make all the difference when technology is used properly. Clearly, technology can be an incredible tool, but it can't replace our teachers and librarians.

With each new technological development, school librarians have had to evolve and modify their roles. We've adapted by adding electronic resources to our print collections, automating our libraries, and embracing the Web in a myriad of ways. It's ironic, however, in this day and age where budget cuts and funding crises are impacting school libraries and schools in general, that we need people more than ever to fill these ever-expanding roles. While technology can improve productivity, it's not lessening the number of people we need in these positions. Instead of just managing books and magazines, school librarians have to manage books, magazines, CDs, DVDs, websites, full-text databases, digital cameras, and computers; the list goes on and on. Instead of simplifying the job of the school librarian, technology and other changes in the schools have merely lengthened the list of items to attend to on a daily basis.

Beyond knowledge of what technology exists are the more important skills of knowing how to effectively use those tools and the appropriate time to use them. That's one of the crucial roles the school librarian plays. We bring with us a set of skills as both teacher and librarian, technologist and technician, which we can use to bridge the gap between everyone in our schools. We're a point of contact for teachers who need to know how to use equipment in their classrooms, and we're a resource for educating students how to find, evaluate, and use information. On the other hand, knowing when and how to use technology also means that we should recognize when technology isn't the answer. Determining appropriate use and uncovering the myriad of ways that the same task can be completed means allowing students to better apply their own different learning styles to each lesson.

Because technology is always changing, it usually means that we're working with things that are new. While this often brings a sense of excitement for both educators and students alike, it also brings a sense of trepidation. In order to overcome the fear that you may break the equipment or that you won't be able to use the equipment effectively in front of a room of students, you have to immerse yourself in information. Librarians are naturally experts in finding out about things that people want to know. The key is to use that information for yourself. Search for information about the things that you want to know, and learn about new tools and ways of doing things.

More than 77,000 public school library media centers and 17,000 private school library media centers are in the United States. That equates to more than 48 million students.[3] Clearly, what we say and do will have a big impact on this generation of students and what they will take with them into their adult lives. It's the responsibility of the school librarian to ensure that the most appropriate technologies are used effectively in our school libraries. Our teachers and students depend on our guidance.

CHALLENGES

Technology often has the tendency to create new problems even though they may be solving different ones. One of biggest challenges that we have to overcome is information overload. Access to greater amounts of information from more and more diverse places has been a driving force for technology in the library. Of course, our students want to find as much information as they can on their topics, and they want all of the viewpoints and opinions. They want related materials and materials from different sources in order to get a well-rounded representation of references. However, they now have to sort through even greater amounts of information to find what they need. This, in turn, leads students to select resources that may not be the best and even reduces the number of resources they utilize due to having too many choices. Some materials may duplicate others, some are not relevant, and many others need to be evaluated in terms of quality and appropriateness. More of our time is spent on these information literacy skills in order to overcome the glut of information that our students have access to.

Other challenges harken back to the previously mentioned budgetary and staffing issues. While studies now show the importance of the school library and its impact on student learning, administrators and school boards aren't aware of, or worse, choose to ignore, those reports. The result is that school librarians are not valued as much as they should be. It is, therefore, our responsibility to make our names known and to speak loudly about all that we do. We must show how important we are to our schools and that the schools won't thrive without us. Too much time is wasted on tasks that should be handled by support staff so that the school librarians can focus on the bigger issues. Testing and standards, while relevant and important, are pulling the focus from some of the good work that teachers and librarians should be doing.

Student expectations are also a challenge for today's educators. As students become more accustomed to the media-rich television, movie, and video game environment of today, they expect more entertainment in their schools. While there's nothing new about this expectation, the twist is not only that they want the same flashy computer graphics they see at home, but that these students are growing up learning these skills at an early age. Some students know more about these tools than their teachers and librarians, thereby reinforcing the importance of lifelong learning in order to keep up. This can be difficult for some adults who are used to how things are and have a hard time changing. Present-day school librarians and library students didn't grow up with computers and Internet access in their home. We're nonnative speakers in a sense, learning this foreign language of technology as adults. It's much easier for children to gain confidence and skills when they have access to these tools from an early age.

Finally, having all of these choices makes it difficult to determine when and where to allocate resources and how to help students find the information they need. In the past, pulling a book off the shelf or handing a film strip to a teacher was what was needed. Presently, that book could also be complemented with an e-book, a website, a CD-ROM, and on and on. A few filmstrips may still be around, but most likely you'll have a videotape or a DVD or a streaming video off the Web. How do you decide what to purchase? How many different formats do you need? Often, older formats are not disappearing but are instead coexisting with new formats, resulting in a more complex decision tree.

WHAT IS TECHNOLOGY?

The word *library* comes from the Latin word *liber*, which means book. However, the library as it exists today is a far cry from that original repository of books. The library houses not only books, but also many different forms of technology. The definition of technology that *Information Power* refers to is "the theory and practice of design, development, utilization, management and evaluation of processes and resources for learning."[4] That's a broad definition, and one that I agree we need to keep in mind as we consider what technology is, its purpose, and what we can do with it. Books can be considered a type of technology, just as a computer with a Web page can. Technology can include a multimedia projector or an overhead projector with a transparency or simply a whiteboard. Pencils and paper, which seem so low tech today, were considered marvels of progress generations ago when students only had wax tablets.

We must also keep in mind how these different technologies fit into our schools. Some, such as computers, can be viewed as more general in nature.

Computers are not specific to libraries, but the way they are used in a library setting is what librarians have to learn about. You'll find computers in classrooms, in homes, and in businesses. Most technology has this versatile nature, and it's up to us to adapt each piece to our needs and the learning environment. On the other hand, some things such as library automation software truly are specific to libraries, even though they may have similarities to other systems found in the business world.

HISTORY AND STANDARDS

We've come a long way from the earliest technologies such as the clay tablet on which the writer would carefully inscribe with a stylus (2500 B.C.–A.D. 100), papyrus rolls written on with brushes or pens (2000 B.C.–A.D. 700), codexes (A.D. 100), and the development of the printing press (A.D. 1450).[5] Our libraries also look much different, serve a much different purpose, and only vaguely resemble the earliest libraries. Compare, for example, ancient libraries in the Sumerian city of Uruk (circa 3000 B.C.), Sumerian Ur (circa 2600 B.C.), and Alexandria (circa 283 B.C.)[6] to the present-day Library of Congress, Online Computer Library Center (OCLC), or any of your school libraries.

More relevant to us are developments such as the introduction of the Dewey Decimal Classification system by Melvil Dewey in 1876 and the foundation of the American Library Association by Melvil Dewey, Justin Winsor, and William Frederick Poole in the same year. In 1898, the New York State Library School offered the first elective in children's librarianship, followed in 1901 by the Carnegie Library of Pittsburgh's development of specialized training for children's librarians.[7] From here, we see the influence of schools and educating students take hold. In 1914, the American Association of School Librarians (AASL) was founded at the American Library Association (ALA) Midwinter Meeting. There the council approved a petition from the ALA Roundtable of Normal and High School Librarians to form a School Libraries section. At the 1915 ALA Annual Conference, the section held its first meeting and elected its first president, Mary Hall, who was librarian at Girls' High School, Brooklyn.

The first standards for secondary school libraries were developed by what was then the Committee on Library Organization and Equipment of the National Educational Association and then published by the ALA in 1920. The Association for Educational Communications and Technology (AECT), the closely related partner to AASL, was founded soon after in 1923.

It wasn't until October 4, 1957, when the Soviet Union launched the first satellite, Sputnik, into orbit, that school libraries started to develop a greater technology component. At that time, America feared that the Soviets had passed our nation in the space race. In response, Congress set up the National Defense Education Act in 1958 to strengthen science and mathematics instruction in the public schools. Title III funding was provided to purchase hardware for public schools. Under the Eisenhower administration an increased push for technological changes in schools and their libraries began.

The 1960s saw continued growth and change. The 1960 *Standards for School Library Programs* by the AASL expanded the scope of the school library program to include audiovisual materials, the first time that incorporating technology is clearly mandated as part of school librarians' responsibilities. This coincided with the growth of school library programs nationwide, with additional federal funding, and with the influential Knapp School Libraries Project promoting the development of school library collections. In 1969, the joint committee of the AASL and the Department of Audiovisual Instruction of the National Education Association (now the AECT) prepared the first joint standards for school media programs.[8] This was a major indication of the changing role of the school librarian. It introduced the terms *media, media specialist, media center,* and *media program* into our vocabulary. By their definition, media was "printed and audiovisual forms of communication and their accompanying technology."[9]

While *school library media specialist* is the most commonly used title today, there's still widespread use of other terms such as *school librarian, teacher librarian,* and more. Some students may even use the title *library teacher* since it has a familiar ring that fits into children's schema, similar to *art teacher, music teacher,* and others. Regardless of the actual term used, the introduction of the term *media* in the 1969 standards set in place a major change.

Personally, I have a bias toward using the term *school librarian* or simply *librarian.* In the library world, we generally classify librarians as academic, public, school, or special, with a few other specialties that may include medical, law, and so forth. Everyone knows what a librarian is, so why not just leave it as that? If you really need to modify it with a specialty, why not just add *school*? But that's a matter of preference, and the debate continues.

In the 1980s, the school library starts looking recognizable to today's students. It was then that computers were becoming affordable and the first computerized automation systems started replacing the card catalog. While those early systems were rudimentary by today's expectations and there are still smaller school libraries that aren't yet automated, overall these changes were taking place at a rapid pace.

Around this time, school librarians realized that they needed to come together and focus on a fresh look at the profession. With those thoughts in mind, the ALA and the AECT developed the first *Information Power* text in 1988. The book contains the first time that guidelines mention access to information outside of the physical library through the searching of online databases.[10] *Information Power* also describes instruction in the operation of equipment, and the use of information in various formats.[11]

With such a positive response to the 1988 *Information Power* and the rapidly changing environment, the ALA and the Association for Educational Communications and Technology revised and updated the guidelines for the current 1998 edition. These guidelines can be found in school libraries and library science classrooms around the country. It's hard to imagine that there are any school librarians who haven't read or at least skimmed this book; it's become the basis for what's taught in graduate-level school library media classes.

The 1998 *Information Power* focuses on three main themes as a foundation for our field: collaboration, leadership, and technology.[12] Here we see the progression of technology in the school library reaching its pinnacle. Technology has moved from being nonexistent, or at a minimum not recognized, to being a small part of our jobs, to being the core of who we are and what we do.

Most recently, the AASL 2007 *Standards for the 21st Century Learner* focuses on technology skills as crucial for future employment needs. Technology is threaded through all four areas:[13]

1) Inquire, think critically, and gain knowledge
2) Draw conclusions, make informed decisions, apply knowledge to new situations, and create new knowledge
3) Share knowledge and participate ethically and productively as members of our democratic society
4) Pursue personal and aesthetic growth

The additional role of instructional design in which school librarians are seen as instructional consultants blends together with the need to collaborate with teachers in creating rich learning environments for our students. Reaching out to the classroom teachers can include basic library skills instruction, teaching information literacy, providing resources, and developing instructional lessons and units that tie into the curriculum. It also includes helping teachers in the use of technology and in integrating technology into their classes and lessons. The school librarian is in the ideal position to interact with school personnel at just about every level. As *Information Power* states, "The library media specialist is a primary leader in the school's use of all kinds of technologies—both instructional and informational—to enhance learning."[14]

Finally, it's important to understand that there is a difference between maintaining technology and using it effectively. *Information Power* again clarifies this point in stating, "Acting as a technologist (rather than a technician) and a collaborator with teachers, the library media specialist plays a critical role in designing student experiences that focus on authentic learning, information literacy, and curricular mastery—not simply on manipulating machinery."[15] This is an important concept to understand. While most school librarians certainly have to deal with the day-to-day tasks of troubleshooting and maintaining equipment and the actual responsibilities will vary from school to school, time and energy should be focused on higher-level activities.

ABOUT THIS BOOK

The purpose of this book is to provide an overview of the types of technologies in use in school libraries, ranging from the more traditional low-tech options to the latest developments. This book also includes information on how the school librarian interacts and works with the technology, providing a detailed picture of how a school librarian can build a technology-rich library. How technology use in the library impacts teachers and students throughout the school and how the school librarian can use technology to improve student learning are part of this discussion.

The technology continues to change so rapidly that books become out of date very quickly. There are many other excellent resources that school librarians have and can refer to. This book provides a foundation on which to build. I hope that school librarians and others in education will remain diligent in staying on top of changes by reading current journal articles, blogs, websites, tweets, and other means of communication.

The audience for this book consists of practicing school librarians, library science graduate students, and library support staff. A secondary set of interested readers includes school administrators, technology coordinators, and teachers. While readers may proceed through the book cover to cover, some may choose to skip around to specific chapters that interest them or that contain needed information.

The book is separated into five parts. The first part provides a basic overview of the information tools that make up the building blocks of a school library. The hardware and software choices, desktop computers, networks, and productivity software, while common in many other settings and environments, set the stage for library-specific activities and additional library-related needs.

The second part discusses information resources in the school library. These chapters cover the different varieties of educational software available, resources available via the Web, and the importance of creating your own school library website.

The third part moves from the library to other parts of the school. These chapters talk about the tools that you can use in the classroom and how you can get involved with students outside of the library.

The fourth part is technology administration. This includes automation, filters and security on student computers, library security systems, and the creation of technology plans in order to look to the future.

The final part of this book covers technology and specific teaching aspects in order to make use of the school library throughout the curriculum. This includes a chapter on in-services and continuing education for teachers, as well as a chapter on the production of handouts and other materials for students and teachers. It concludes with a new chapter for this second edition by wrapping up with an overview of Web 2.0 technologies and the tools that allow greater collaboration than ever before.

My hope is that by the end, the reader will have a stronger sense of the types of technology in use in school libraries. While individual library budgets and other factors may mean that your specific library may look much different than another, at least you'll be aware of the possibilities and how to effectively use what you do have.

WEBSITES

American Association of School Librarians: www.ala.org/aasl

American Library Association: www.ala.org

Association for Educational Communications and Technology: www.aect .org

Association for Library and Information Science Education Youth Services Special Interest Group: https://mywebspace.wisc.edu/smcqueen/web/alise/youth_services/

NOTES

1. American Association of School Librarians and Association for Educational Communications and Technology, *Information Power: Building Partnerships for Learning* (Chicago: American Library Association, 1998), 126.

2. Missouri Department of Elementary and Secondary Education, "Show-Me Connection: An Additional Study on the Relationship between School Library Media Services and Student Achievement," www.dese.state.mo.us/divimprove/curriculum/librarystudy/ libraryresearch2.pdf (accessed June 22, 2004).

3. U.S. Department of Education, National Center for Education Statistics, *The Status of Public and Private School Library Media Centers in the United States: 1999–2000*, NCES 2004-313, ed. Barbara Holton, Yupin Bae, Susan Baldridge, Michelle

Brown, and Dan Heffron (Washington, DC: U.S. Department of Education 2004), vii. http://nces.ed.gov/pubs2004/2004313.pdf (accessed June 3, 2006).

4. Barbara B. Seels and Rita C. Richey, *Instructional Technology: The Definition and Domains of the Field* (Washington, DC: Association for Educational Communications and Technology, 1994), 1.

5. Frederick G. Kilgour, *The Evolution of the Book* (New York: Oxford University Press, 1998), 3–10.

6. Don H. Tolzman, Alfred Hessel, and Reuben Peiss, *The Memory of Mankind: The Stories of Libraries since the Dawn of History* (New Castle, DE.: Oak Knoll Press, 2001), 2–4.

7. June Lester and Kathy H. Latrobe, "The Education of School Librarians," in *The Emerging School Library Media Center: Historical Issues and Perspectives*, ed. Kathy H. Latrobe (Englewood, CO: Libraries Unlimited, 1998), 1–15.

8. American Library Association and National Education Association, *Standards for School Media Programs* (Chicago: American Library Association, 1969), ix–xvi.

9. American Library Association, *Standards for School Media Programs*, xi.

10. American Association of School Librarians and Association for Educational Communications and Technology, *Information Power: Guidelines for School Library Media Programs* (Chicago: American Library Association, 1988), 1.

11. American Association of School Librarians, *Information Power: Guidelines*, 10–12.

12. American Association of School Librarians, *Information Power: Building Partnerships*, 47.

13. American Association of School Librarians, *Standards for the 21st Century Learner* (Chicago: American Library Association, 2007), 1-8.

14. American Association of School Librarians, *Information Power: Building Partnerships*, 54.

15. American Association of School Librarians, *Information Power: Building Partnerships*, 54.

1

INFORMATION TOOLS

1

Hardware

The first part of this book covers basic information tools. This includes underlying structural components like hardware, software, and the network architecture found in your libraries and schools. It provides the background and the basis for much of the more detailed and library-specific technologies that follow.

This chapter covers computers and the most common peripherals: printers and scanners. It provides the details you need to better understand the choices that must be made and to speak more comfortably about library technology needs with administrators, teachers, and other tech people in your schools.

COMPUTERS

Besides shelves of books, what technology do people expect to find in a library? The computer is probably the single most common piece of technology. Alone, the computer is merely a basic tool waiting for a purpose. However, it's the foundation for all the software, databases, websites, and automation systems that are built upon it for library users. Computers have been completely ingrained in society for quite some time, and it's hard to believe that there was a time when we didn't have them. Much of what we discuss later in the book relies on this first piece of technology.

Knowledge about computer specifications is needed to understand current uses for computers that you already have. You need to determine if a particular computer is capable of running software you want to purchase, if the computer is nearing the end of its useful life, and what to look for when buying new computers. Although specifications and requirements change continually, this overview will help.

This chapter focuses on the personal computer (PC) as opposed to the Mac or other options. Although there are still Mac enthusiasts and there's certainly still a niche for Macs, the current and foreseeable future is dominated by the PC, so that's our focus.

Before we talk about the components of the computer, we need to understand that advances in technology have made computer purchases more complicated and simultaneously worry free, an interesting dichotomy. Everyone is aware of running jokes about buying technology only to have it outdated by newer models at lower prices the very next day. Prices do continue to drop and computers do become more powerful every day; they certainly won't last forever. But they've improved so much that their life expectancies have increased, and software hasn't kept up at the same pace in terms of hardware requirements. You don't have to be as worried about buying something not powerful enough because almost any computer will now meet your basic needs. Some effort is required to maximize those decisions, but the mystery of buying a computer isn't what it was 10 or 20 years ago.

The Case

The guts of the computer are enclosed in the main case; everything else is connected to this with cables or wires, or the connection is made wirelessly. The first specification that's usually addressed is the central processing unit (CPU), or processor for short. The two main producers are currently Intel and Advanced Micro Devices (AMD). Each has led in market share only to have the other come out with a new processor and then take over the lead. In general, Intel processors tend to be slightly more expensive, but both provide more than enough power for today's requirements. The top-of-the-line and most expensive processors are only really needed by people working with above-average requirements. You may need a little more power for video editing, for instance, but typical Web browsing does not require anything special.

Processor

Processor speed is often referred to in terms of clock speed. For instance, a 1-GHz processor performs 1 billion operations per second. G (giga) is a prefix indicating 1 billion, and Hz (hertz) refers to cycles or operations. Typical processors today can run up to 3 GHz although between 1 to 2 GHz is more prevalent. However, clock speed is not the only factor. Processor speed overall also depends on the processor cache, a storage area for frequently accessed data, and the frontside bus, the physical connection between the processor and memory. The bus is the speed at which data flows between the processor and the memory. If the processor has to stop and wait for the rest of the computer to catch up, the overall system isn't very efficient. Therefore, you want as fast a bus as you can get to eliminate those bottlenecks. Because these various components determine the actual speed of processing power, Intel and AMD have shifted away from focusing on one overall number and have been using naming schemes that reflect how their processors differ from each other. However, a race to increase the number of cores available on each chip has increased competition again, allowing computers with multiple cores to perform multiple tasks at the same time, as long as the software running has been specifically optimized for such work. This is not always the case.

The Pentium, Celeron, and Core lines include a multitude of varieties by Intel for desktops and laptops. Slightly slower yet requiring less energy are the Atom lines, ideal for netbooks. Similarly, AMD produces an Athlon, quad core, and a Sempron variety. With continually new products, don't be surprised by a new list of names tomorrow.

Any new computer today will have a processor that's fast enough to meet your standard needs. If you buy the fastest computer available, you will pay a premium. Buy the cheapest you can get and it will be outdated a bit faster than average. So shoot for that middle ground. That's where you usually find the best deals. Frankly, any chip you buy today is going to be in the gigahertz range and should meet most of your basic needs.

Hard Drive

The hard drive, where all of your programs and files are stored, is probably the next important component of the case to consider. This one area has far exceeded other areas of computer development. It's rare that anyone actually fills up a hard drive any longer because there's usually more space than you need. Of course, it's also easy to upgrade and replace a hard drive with a newer and larger one if you really need to, and external hard drives are now easy to purchase. The typical hard drive in the 75- to 100-GB range offers more storage than most need for all of their programs. The newest and largest hard drives offer up to 1 TB of storage, which most schools will never need, especially because storage space of that size may simply reside on the network. The only time that you might need more than average would be if you were doing a great deal of video editing or storing down-loaded video files. Most of your library and classroom computers won't be doing this, but if you do have some video-editing stations, then a large hard drive would be beneficial. Other activities, such as working with still images, accessing the Web, and using educational software programs, tend to take up relatively little space.

There are differences in terms of hard drive speed, but for our typical uses a faster speed doesn't make that much of an impact. A 7200-rpm (revolutions per minute) hard drive with an 8-MB buffer is ideal.

Generally, you want to leave about 20 percent of the hard drive free. If you start filling it up beyond that, you might run into problems. As programs are running, temporary files are constantly being written to the hard drive, so extra space must be left for that processing to continue. If the programs and files are taking up too much space, then you'll need to think about upgrading to a new computer, purchasing a larger hard drive, or adding an additional hard drive. With hard drive prices now dropping to $1 per gigabyte or less, you can easily buy as much space as you need.

Memory

Random-access memory (RAM) is the final internal component in the computer case that largely determines the computer's capabilities. It's also the easiest to upgrade and replace yourself. Before buying additional RAM, check the specifications for that computer. There are many different types of RAM and using the wrong type in your computer will at best, not work, and at worst, permanently damage the computer.

RAM is the working memory of the computer. It takes information from the hard drive as determined by the computer user's input, and the processor uses this temporary and fast memory space to work on the request. Increasing the amount of RAM effectively increases the speed of the computer. It's usually the cheapest and easiest way to increase performance. To determine the amount of RAM that you require, check the specifications from all of the different programs that you run on that computer. Unless you're doing something very intensive such as video editing or high end graphics, an average amount of RAM should do just fine. Windows XP requires 512 MB minimum, but usually runs better with at least 1 GB of RAM. Windows Vista and Windows 7 are similar, requiring 1 GB minimum, with 2 GB being preferred. As a side note, students who play a lot of intensive video games at home may have up to 4 GB of RAM because of the complex graphical functions. If your school cannot afford new library computers, then adding RAM is a way to upgrade so that the older computers are still usable. Technically, today's 32-bit processors allow a maximum of 4 GB of RAM, and 64-bit processors allow up to 128 GB. These are the theoretical limits because the number of slots available for RAM varies by make and model. Furthermore, these amounts are overkill on desktop and laptop

PCs and are more important for high-use servers that handle a great deal of traffic.

Other Components

In addition to these components, be sure that the computer has a decent sound card. Though sound cards are standard, verify that one is included. In the past, sound wasn't seen as important and sound from an entire computer lab was viewed as disruptive, but we can always control when sound is on or off. You'll also want to be sure that the computer has a network card. Again, most computers come network ready, but ensure that they're compatible with your specifics. If not, network cards are easily replaced and upgraded. Ease of replacement is also true of the power supply and fans. Although hard drives do crash occasionally and RAM can go bad, they and the rest of the internal components are extremely resilient nowadays. If anything goes it's often something as simple as a fan. Fans are important to lower the temperature because processors create a large amount of heat. If the fan malfunctions, then the computer will get too hot and shut down. It's inexpensive and easy to replace the fan yourself if this ever happens.

Monitors

Today's monitors can last longer than the computer itself, but because of lowering prices and package deals, most people buy a monitor and a computer together. This also reduces the chance that the monitor will die before the new computer, and it makes warranty issues easier to resolve.

Flat-screen liquid crystal display (LCD) monitors are now the norm compared to the larger cathode-ray tubes (CRTs), which dominated until just a few short years ago. There'll come a point very soon when CRTs simply won't exist.

CRTs work like the older standard TV. A beam of electrons is shot at phosphor dots on the inside of a glass tube. This produces dots of red, green, or blue light. These monitors come in a variety of resolutions and give the best look to full-motion video. However, they take up the most desk space and are the heaviest to physically pick up and move.

In the screen of an LCD monitor, each pixel is produced by a tiny cell that contains a thin layer of liquid crystals. The main benefits are thinner and lighter displays and decreased use of electricity. Some of the older-model or less-expensive LCDs have slower refresh rates (the time it takes for the computer to redraw a changed image on the screen), so video that moves too quickly won't display as clearly because the screen appears to flicker. A refresh rate of 75 Hz is the minimum you would want. Furthermore, some LCDs are difficult to view from an angle, making it hard for multiple students to look at the screen simultaneously. However, these problems are improving with each new generation of LCDs. Dot pitch refers to the distance between the dots on the screen; the smaller the distance, the sharper the image. Today, the standard dot pitch is at or less than 0.26 mm.

Monitor sizes of 17 inches have become the new standard, with 15-inch monitors selling less and less. Anything smaller has a difficult time displaying the interfaces and environments of today's software. Monitors above 17 inches make viewing much easier for the user, but price makes them rarer in today's schools and libraries. Unless you have stations for video editing, publishing software for something like a school newspaper, or students with vision problems who need a larger screen for larger fonts, then a 17-inch monitor should do just fine.

Drives

In order for boxed software to be installed on your computers and for students to save files that they want to take home with them, storage media drives have to be included. There are two main types: magnetic and optical.

Magnetic drives work by having the drive head come in contact with a slowly spinning flexible disk. These disks are prone to damage and wear and tear, but they are a mature technology that everyone is aware of.

The basic magnetic drive that most people remember is the 3½-inch floppy disk. Holding only 1.44 MB, it doesn't keep up with today's needs. It can hold a small word-processed file and a few small images. You can still add an external floppy drive via a USB (Universal Serial Bus) cable, but the end of the floppy is here.

Other magnetic drives that work on the same principles but contain more storage space include the Zip disk by Iomega. Although they are physically larger than the floppy disk and therefore not compatible, they come in 100-, 250-, or 750-MB versions.

Current trends in file transfer and storage are dominated by the USB flash drive. With no moving parts but still working on a magnetic principle, these small devices have continued to drop in price and increase in storage size on an almost weekly basis. Inexpensive devices can be purchased for only a few dollars, making them ideal for children to pick up like any other school supplies at the start of the year. Because a USB port in the front of the computer is all that's needed to use the flash drive, the student can be sure of the interchangeability and interoperability of their storage device between school and home. On a related note, small laptops and netbooks are now sometimes offered with flash memory in place of a hard drive. Although still more expensive, there is a benefit in terms of power savings and size.

Optical drives work on the principles of lasers reading microscopic pits burned into the inner layers of the disk. The disk is covered with clear plastic to protect the data. The CD is a standard optical drive and should be included in any computer you purchase today. It's needed most often for installing and running software programs.

Because prices have dropped, you might have writable and/or rewritable CD drives on your computers. They've become so common that it's actually difficult not to get one nowadays.

CD-Rs (recordable) are disks that you can write to a single time for backup and storage purposes. The disks are extremely cheap, have write speeds 32 times faster than earlier models, and make for quick burning (recording). Instead of creating an actual pit as the traditional CD burner, these drives work by the use of a special laser that interacts with a photosensitive dye. The laser alters the dye to create a series of light and dark dots that effectively create a similar series of on and off sections for the data to be recorded to.

CD-RW (rewritable) disks use a different chemical that can be changed back and forth repeatedly, effectively making them reusable for thousands of times. You'll notice on the drive that it has specific speeds at which it will write, erase, and read. You'll be hard pressed to find a computer that doesn't include a rewritable drive today. Both CD-R and CD-RW disks hold about 650 MB.

DVD drives are also extremely common today, and you'll probably want to include them so that movies and other media with high-storage content can be viewed. DVDs work on the same principles as the CD except that it uses a finer laser to read smaller pits that are closer together. A single-layer DVD can hold 4.7 GB and a double layer 8.5 GB. DVD-RW drives have also come down in price, and if you're doing anything with video editing you might want to consider purchasing these as well. Otherwise, a standard DVD drive should be just fine.

There are a plethora of newer technologies. Blu-ray, the next replacement for the CD and the DVD drives, uses a blue laser instead of the red. By using a smaller wavelength, the burner can pack more information onto the same size disk—up to 23 GB of data. This is ideal for either high-definition video or for greater standard video capacity.

Sound Devices

As the applications that students use and multimedia on the Web becomes more and more prevalent, library and classroom computers need to have sound devices. Output devices, such as speakers and headphones, should be acquired if not packaged with the computer. Speakers are ideal if students are working together in a group since they don't cut the student off from others. Headphones, on the other hand, allow a student to work privately and closely listen to audio that may disturb others. A combination of the two is ideal, depending on the setup. Additionally, an input device such as a microphone is important if there are specific programs or projects wherein students need to record their own voices.

Other Items

Standard items that you'll need with a computer include a keyboard and a mouse. These decisions are usually made for you since such standard devices are included with all computers. As an upgrade or a later add-on, you can purchase keyboards that are designed for ergonomics and keyboards that are wireless. However, a standard and inexpensive keyboard is all you need. As for the mouse, an optical mouse without a track ball is ideal. Students in the past would sometimes remove the track ball as a prank, and the track balls can also get jammed with dirt and dust. Optical mice are slightly more expensive but have become the standard.

You'll also want a computer with multiple USB ports in the front. USB ports are standard on computers today. There are usually a couple in the back for connecting printers and other items and a couple in the front for use with digital cameras, USB flash drives, and other portable devices.

Finally, you'll want to have proper surge protectors. There are probably existing protectors in place if you are replacing computers, but it's something that's often overlooked and forgotten about until you start trying to plug everything in.

PRINTERS

As with any computer, you'll need a way to print out information that students find. While almost nonexistent, dot matrix printers can still be found at a few circulation desks. Otherwise, laser printers and color ink jet printers are much more common in school libraries.

Dot Matrix

Dot matrix printers are based on typewriter technology in which a series of pins strike an ink ribbon transferring the dots of ink to paper. These printers can range from 9 to 24 pins; the higher the number of pins, the sharper the final image. About the only place that you'll find dot matrix printers is near a circulation desk. They're good for printing text quickly and inexpensively. However, with the newer Web- and Windows-based circulation systems now in place, even dot matrix printers are quickly disappearing.

Laser Printers

Monochrome laser printers are common. They work on the same electrostatic principle that photocopies are based on. Toner is relatively inexpensive, print outs are fast, and images are sharp. They work best on text and simple graphics, although they have a difficult time with printing photographic images because black and white prints of color images do not translate perfectly. However, laser printers have come down in price and are the standard printer in libraries. Depending on your use, you'll need to decide if extra paper trays are necessary to reduce the number of times they need to be refilled and if you want to pay more for a faster printer.

Color

Color inkjet printers have populated the home office, but the high cost of printing cartridges and their slower speed has not made them as practical in the library. They work by spraying a fine series of dots in a combination of cyan, magenta, and yellow to create all of the colors in the image. Slightly higher-end printers will also have a separate black cartridge. The drawback is that these printers are extremely slow and use a lot of expensive ink. Some color inkjet printers can be outfitted with tubing to connect large economy-size ink bottles external to the printer. By purchasing in bulk, the ink is much less expensive and refilling is required less often. A library might want to have a color printer as an option for someone who really needs an occasional color printout.

Color laser printers are the newest technology. They produce must faster printouts and are much higher quality. However, they're still generally too expensive for libraries, although this is quickly changing. Although initially more expensive, the color laser saves money in the long run with less-expensive toner.

SCANNERS

Although digital cameras have reduced the need for scanners, there are still times when an object needs to be physically scanned. In the library, uses may include digitizing older pictures from film, student handmade artwork, historical print documents, etc. These images may be incorporated into the library website or for use in student projects.

The two main types of scanners are flatbed and handheld. The flatbed scanner allows the user to place the sheet of paper on the glass of the scanner and then close the lid to keep it in place and to provide a neutral background so that only the image gets picked up. Similar to a photocopy machine in handling the paper, the scanning process is simple to initiate and is ideal for standard-sized paper. The handheld scanner, on the other hand, is a small device that the user can manipulate across the paper. It's ideal for small, quick scanning projects and, therefore, is often used in addition to flatbed scanners instead of in place of them.

Scanners work by use of a charge-coupled device that transfers the image of the object into a digital form. Quality of images is measured in terms of bit depth. The minimum you would want is 24-bit depth, meaning that each pixel provides eight bits of information for each of the three colors: red, blue, and green. This translates to about 16 million colors providing photographic quality. In terms of optical resolution, you would want 300 dpi (dots per inch) minimum for clarity of the image on the computer screen and for quality of the printed image.

Scanners usually come with their own basic software packages to handle simple manipulation of images. Since 1992, the TWAIN standard for communication between software and hardware has been in place across the industry.

Additional software can provide more flexibility and uses. One type of software is optical character recognition (OCR), which converts text images to a text file that can be edited and manipulated in a word processor. One of the more popular software packages is Adobe Acrobat. Acrobat turns full-page images into portable document format (PDF) files. Anyone can download the free PDF viewer to view your scanned images exactly as the originals appear, regardless of the software that was used to originally create the document. To manipulate and edit scanned images, you need an art program, such as Adobe Photoshop, the less-expensive Jasc Paint Shop Pro, or the free, open-source GIMP.

Scanners today usually connect to computers via USB cables. If you have an older computer, you might have problems using newer scanners because of this USB connection mode and because scanners are memory intensive. Older scanners were difficult to use, but modern scanners and computers are much easier. It's not like using a photocopier; be prepared to spend time when scanning. This is why little scanning is done in general, and large collections are digitizing only when many people have a lot of time. However, this is a good place to train students or to get volunteers involved.

HOW MANY DO I NEED?

Determining the number of computers needed will naturally vary from school to school. Ideally, you want a circulation computer and a separate computer for the librarian. You'll then want several computers for students to search the OPAC (online public access catalog), the Web, and databases;

computers for multimedia programs and educational software, such as encyclopedias on CD; and a stand-alone computer for programs like Accelerated Reader. In a perfect world, you would have one computer per student for general use, based upon the expected number of students you might have in the library at one time. As more computers are placed in the classrooms, you might find that student visits to the library decrease because they can access library materials from their classrooms. However, there will always be a need for a computer classroom to teach an entire class at once, so you'll need a lab that can fit an entire class. If you can't afford one computer per student, then two students per computer would work.

In terms of printers, the librarian's computer and the circulation computer need to be able to print. If located close together, they could share a networked laser printer. An additional color printer would also be nice for producing colorful handouts and displays. For students, a heavy-duty laser printer with an extra paper tray could cover an entire computer classroom and another could cover the rest of the library.

A single flatbed scanner would be a good start. Anything more than that would only be necessary if some of the teachers in your school have specific units and projects that require all of the students in a class to do a lot of scanning.

MAINTENANCE AND RESPONSIBILITY

Each school has their own policies and procedures for working with technology. It's a good idea to determine where specific responsibilities lie. Larger schools probably have dedicated tech people who handle installation and maintenance. However, the school librarian is in the ideal place to help teachers and students in the use of technology and in basic troubleshooting. Especially in the smaller schools, the librarian can take on more of these technical issues. Regardless of who else is involved with the technology, be sure that you always have the option of working with your own equipment. Librarians should be given administrator rights to download, install, and maintain their own equipment—even if tech people are hired to do this.

There's been considerable discussion regarding the amount of waste produced worldwide because of this endless cycle of purchasing new technology to replace old, outdated equipment. Many of the components include harmful chemicals and metals that can leach into water supplies if they're dumped into our landfills. Therefore, proper handling of older equipment means recycling or selling what is no longer needed. Because most schools have mandates that don't allow them to sell equipment, or books for that matter, to the general public, many have turned to sending out bids to companies that handle the processing of old equipment. Although it won't bring in a lot of money to the school, every dollar helps. These companies take entire pallets of equipment at a time and either recycle the parts or sell them to other interested parties.

WEBSITES

Advanced Micro Devices: www.amd.com/
Adobe Acrobat: www.adobe.com/products/acrobat
Adobe Photoshop: www.adobe.com/products/photoshop
CNET: www.cnet.com
GIMP: www.gimp.org
Jasc Paint Shop Pro: www.jasc.com/products/paintshoppro
Intel Corporation: www.intel.com
PC Technology Guide: www.pctechguide.com
PC World: www.pcworld.com/reviews
ZDNet: www.zdnet.com

2

Software

Although some software is specifically intended for libraries and education, software in any context relies on standardized underlying operating systems that computers require to function. Basic productivity suites, antivirus software, graphics software, and Web browsers are usually installed on most, if not all, library computers. These programs make up what we consider a base install. This will get your computers up and running, and then you'll be able to tailor them to your library's needs. Therefore, these decisions must be made initially.

Because very few people get the opportunity to build a library with all new equipment, you'll most likely be working with equipment and software inherited from a previous librarian or from elsewhere in the building or district. Nonetheless, with technology (especially software), nothing lasts forever. At some point, you'll need to upgrade and replace software and hardware. This chapter provides you with some underlying decisions and assumptions that you'll encounter. Furthermore, keep in mind that some of these decisions are handled differently from school to school. Some of you may have complete control over these options and some of you may not have any. Regardless, you need to be aware of the options, and you need to talk with the people involved in the decision making. Even if you have the authority to make computer purchases, there'll be many others to work with. Although it's not always possible, it's usually best to have the entire school on similar software for compatibility and maintenance. This requires that you work closely with everyone involved.

OPERATING SYSTEMS

All personal computers (PCs) require an operating system. This underlying structure allows the user to interact with the computer and vice versa. The operating system you choose impacts decisions about other software that you can use on that computer. Software will state system requirements on the package and/or on their website.

You should already know what operating system is on your computers because the name appears every time you turn the computer on. As soon as you hit the power button, this software takes over and starts reading from the computer's read-only memory (ROM). From there, the Basic Input/Output Systems kicks in and the computer boots up. The operating system's tasks, in the most general sense, fall into six categories:

- Processor management
- Memory management
- Device management
- Storage management
- Application interface
- User interface

The first five tasks are behind the scenes but are very important for you in terms of determining what software will or won't work on your computer. The user interface is clearly an important factor because students have to interact with the computer via the interface you provide. For students who have little computer experience or aren't comfortable working with computers, the usability of the interface can make a big difference in terms of their success.

Your choice of operating system might not be in your control. The majority of schools and businesses today use a Microsoft Windows operating system. Of course, there's a definite niche for Macintosh, Linux, and other options, but over the last decade Microsoft has clearly dominated. What's important is that you're informed and keep up with current trends so that you can speak with administrators and tech people about the direction of library and school computers.

In terms of functionality, all of the following choices have their own unique benefits and drawbacks and are surprisingly similar in terms of functionality. However, there may be differences in terms of cost, software that can be used, and the comfort level of those using and maintaining the computer.

The choice of an operating system is probably something that most people don't even think about. The assumption is that any new computer comes with Microsoft Windows. This is why Microsoft has such a large base and why people are naturally hesitant to change. Because your installed base of existing computers has probably been satisfactory, you'll want to research alternatives very seriously if you decide to make any changes. You'll also want to have support and feedback from administrators and others within the school. The computers in the library should be part of a technology plan based on long-range goals.

Microsoft Windows

Most people use Microsoft Windows. Not always regarded as the very best operating system available, Windows has improved and just about everyone is familiar with it. Most people use it because that's what they're used to, it came with the computer, they fear switching to something else, or because that's what the school now supports.

Not surprisingly, a lot of people are still using older versions of Windows, whether that be Windows 95, 98, ME, or 2000.[1] It's still possible to walk into a school library and see student computers running Windows 95 with hard drive sizes in the megabyte range and RAM (random-access memory) of 32 MB or less. With a tight budget, it can be hard to justify the time and expense to upgrade, and computers in school tend to be used as long as possible. Furthermore, older computers most likely don't have the processing power, memory, and technical requirements needed to run Windows 7, Vista or even XP, so even if you wanted to upgrade, you wouldn't be able to. Furthermore, Windows XP has been stable for so long and Vista has had numerous problems, so most schools are completely skipping Vista and keeping XP running until its necessary to move to Windows 7.

To ensure that your operating system is up-to-date and safe, you need to be sure that you're installing the latest updates. Microsoft regularly provides patches to their software that you'll want to be sure to install.[2] It's important to download and install these patches as soon as the computer is connected to the Internet. It'll be only a matter of minutes before viruses and worms try to attack your computer.

These patches come in three main categories:

High Priority—Crucial updates, security updates, service packs, and update rollups that should be installed as soon as they become available and before you install any other updates

Software (Optional)—Noncrucial fixes for such Windows programs as Windows Media® Player and Windows Journal Viewer

Hardware (Optional)—Noncritical fixes for drivers and other hardware devices, such as video cards, sound cards, scanners, printers, and cameras

It's strongly recommended that you turn on the Automatic Update feature to install the patches as soon as possible. However, you can still do this manually by visiting the Microsoft Windows Update website if you prefer having more direct control.

You must consider myriad options as you set up the library computers. For instance, do you want to keep the monitors on at all times so that they're ready as soon as a student sits down (Power Options under the Control Panel), or will you use a screen saver or power conservation mode? Do students have to log in, or will a generic student account be set as the default?

Apple

While Macs have historically had a strong influence in education, graphics, and a few other niches, they have quite a small market share compared to Microsoft. Mac enthusiasts swear by the quality of these machines, their speed, and their ease of use. On the other hand, they tend to be more expensive, which is difficult to justify when budgets are tight.[3] Day by day, schools that were once populated by Macs are switching to PCs when they buy new. Of course, you can still get by with Macs, but you just have to be aware of compatibility issues and know that you'll be in the minority.

Linux

Apple sales have been minimal because the hardware is tied to its operating system. Linux, on the other hand, is a separate operating system that will work on any PC that currently has Windows. In fact, this open-source solution can be run on slower and older machines than the bloated Windows systems require.[4] Additionally, Linux is free (or at least lower cost) and you'll see why its market share has been slowly increasing over the past few years.

As an open-source environment in which the development and use of the software is free for you to manipulate, the Linux software can be downloaded at no cost. However, many companies have jumped into the market providing their own additions to the Linux operating system along with manuals and support. Otherwise, you're on your own. Some of the options include Red Hat, SuSe, and Mandrake. Additionally, the up and coming Google Chromium, a Linux-based OS, may help to shake up some of Microsoft's stability.

The cost savings is one of the main reasons that people are making the switch to Linux.[5] If you can save money on the software and get by with older machines, then you'll have more money for other software products, books, and journals. Additionally, some people feel that Linux systems are more stable than Windows, meaning fewer crashes and technical problems.

Furthermore, some specific Linux options are available for the K–12 environment. There's a tailor-made Linux operating system that has been purposely created to save schools money.[6] By using thin clients, these inexpensive terminals provide a lot more than what you could get with a regular Windows PC. Other companies, such as the DiscoverStation, have stepped into the fray.[7] The idea is that computers today have more power than is usually used, so by sharing processing power among multiple monitors and input devices, resources can be stretched further.

PRODUCTIVITY SUITES

Once you've chosen an operating system, you'll need to have some type of productivity suite for doing just the basics. This includes a word processor, a spreadsheet, and a presentation product. It could include database, drawing, or other software, but the basics will allow students to type papers, manipulate numbers and data, and present information to teachers and each other. Options here are plentiful also.

Microsoft Office

Microsoft Office is by the far the most popular product in use today and has made the transition to a newer XML-based product.[8] Microsoft maintains that their latest version, Office 2010, ensures the least number of compatibility issues when students are trying to take materials between the library and the classroom and home. Academic pricing means that it's slightly less expensive than the standard product price, but it's still expensive. Nonetheless, some people feel that if a product is so commonly used, then we need to teach the students to be comfortable using it or they'll be left behind. On the other hand, Office's many features can overwhelm students—especially when they only use a fraction of what it offers. Librarians also have to decide what their students need; an elementary school may not need the full Microsoft Office suite, but a high school might justify its use in preparation for college and the work force.

StarOffice and OpenOffice

If you really want to save some money, then open source is again the way to go. Just as Linux has been the open-source alternative for operating systems, OpenOffice is the productivity suite option. This product has made remarkable technical advances and is very similar in most respects to Microsoft Office. There are a few less features, but the majority of the students in a K–12 setting don't really need anything more. Ninety-eight percent of the features in Microsoft Office are never used and are therefore overkill.[9] Many educators firmly believe that OpenOffice will be a dominant player in the future. Sun's StarOffice is based on OpenOffice but has a few additional features available (similar to some of the companies that sell tweaked versions of Linux) and is therefore not free, but its cost is extremely low compared to Microsoft Office. This is a great option for schools or individuals wanting to save money by not buying Microsoft Office while still getting the manuals, support, and compatibility with other products.

WordPerfect and Others

There are, of course, many other options available. WordPerfect was once the leader in productivity suites until Microsoft came along and skillfully dominated the market. Some argue that WordPerfect still creates an equal if not better product. If you're looking for something that can do what Microsoft does, with support and manuals, then you do have some options. It might, however, take some shopping around to find the best prices and the best features for your needs.

ANTIVIRUS

Antivirus software is a must. Whether or not you allow students to access e-mail, there are still other ways that viruses can be contracted. You can become infected from visiting websites or by simply being connected to the Internet and not doing anything. Any time that you have an Internet connection or are transferring files via a removable device like a USB flash drive, you run the threat of a virus getting through. In order to prevent infection, you need antivirus software continually running, you must keep it up-to-date by installing new virus definitions as they become available, and you must ensure that students can't disable or turn off the software.

Two popular products include Symantec Norton AntiVirus and Computer Associates McAfee VirusScan. Either product will do a fine job, and many other options are available.

SPYWARE

Spyware is software that installs on your computer, usually without the user's knowledge or without clearly making the user aware of what it does. Spyware is technically not a virus but instead opens up the computer to tracking and sending statistics to another computer, initiating pop-up advertising, or, worse, allowing a remote computer access to your passwords and other important information. It means that another computer can spy on you and what you're doing. Often little harm is done, but the effects of spyware can add up and slow down the computer or make it completely inoperable. The antivirus makers now include separate software that protects against spyware, or you can get stand-alone spyware tools.

GRAPHICS

One final piece of standard software that you'll want to include on your library computers deals with graphics. Because the use of digital cameras and scanners has become so prevalent and more slideshow presentations are being done by students, they will need a way to manipulate images. Adobe Photoshop is clearly the premier software package available, but it can be quite pricey.[10] There may be a need for a couple licenses if you want to use it yourself, if a few teachers want to use it regularly, or if some older high school students are working on the yearbook or in a graphics-intensive class. Jasc Paint Shop Pro is a less-expensive alternative that can handle many basic tasks. Finally, an excellent free open-source alternative is GIMP.

WEB BROWSER

A good Web browser is necessary to access the library databases, websites, the library catalog, and so much more. Almost any current browser will be satisfactory, but there are many differences of opinions and strong feelings about one or another. While Mosaic, the first Web browser, and many others have come and gone, there are still several options.

Once again, Microsoft has dominated the field with Internet Explorer. This is largely because it is preinstalled or bundled with Microsoft Windows. The majority of computer users simply don't have the time, interest, or comfort level to download or obtain another browser. However, Microsoft has been continually hit with a variety of viruses and security attacks, thereby making alternative browsers more attractive. Internet Explorer has also been criticized for not staying in the forefront of technical development.

Netscape Navigator, once a leader in the browser war, has seen its market share disappear over the years because of Microsoft bundling. Today, Firefox, Google Chrome, and Apples' Safari are seeing increased usage as they innovate and continually improve features to meet new demands.

Because these browsers are free to download, you won't have to worry about incurring additional costs. The browser wars, once thought to be over, are revving up again.

There are, of course, numerous other Web browsers that you can purchase. Some of these, like Opera, have a special niche that they're trying to fill. This includes an entire set of browsers specifically designed for people with disabilities. While the cost of Web browsers is not that expensive, the open-source products will, in the long run, most likely dominate the future.

WEBSITES

Ad-Aware: www.lavasoftusa.com
Adobe Photoshop: www.adobe.com/products/photoshop
Apple: www.apple.com
Corel: www.corel.com
Firefox: www.mozilla.com/firefox/central
FreeOS.com: www.freeos.com
GIMP: www.gimp.org
Google Chrome: www.google.com/chrome
How Stuff Works: http://computer.howstuffworks.com/operating-system
    .htm
Jasc Paint Shop Pro: www.jasc.com/products/paintshoppro
Linux: www.linux.org
Microsoft: www.microsoft.com
Microsoft Windows Update: http://windowsupdate.microsoft.com
Mozilla: www.mozilla.org
Netscape: http://netscape.aol.com
OpenOffice: www.openoffice.org
Opera: www.opera.com
Redhat: www.redhat.com
Spybot: www.safer-networking.org/en/home/index.html
SpywareBlaster: www.javacoolsoftware.com/spywareblaster.html
StarOffice: wwws.sun.com/software/star/staroffice

NOTES

1. Robin Peek, "The Battle of the Windows," *Information Today* 21, no. 2 (February 2004): 15–16.

2. Adam Boettiger, "Tips and Techniques with Windows XP," *Nebraska Library Association Quarterly* 34, no. 2 (Summer 2003): 22–27.

3. Claudia Kienzle, "Mac Aficionado Turned PC Enthusiast," *EMedia* 16, no. 4 (April 2003 supplement): S9

4. Brian Auger, "Living with Linux," *Library Journal Net Connect* (Spring 2004): 16–18.

5. Andrea Baker and Amy Daniels, "Chicks in Charge," *Library Journal* 129, no. 5 (March 15, 2004): 46.

6. Walter Minkel, "Linux at the Right Price," *School Library Journal* 49, no. 4 (April 2003): 32–33.

7. Kathleen A. Peters, "Drowning in PC Management: Could a Linux Solution Save Us?" *Information Today* 24, no. 6 (June 2004): 6–8, 60–64.

8. Robert J. Boeri, "Office 2003 InfoPath and MS Word Professional," *EContent* 26, no. 11 (November 2003): 17–19.

9. Dave Rensberger, "Fast Track and Free: OpenOffice 1.0," *Searcher* 11, no. 5 (May 2003): 46–48.

10. Jan Ozer, "The Power and Influence of Photoshop," *EMedia* 16, no. 10 (October 2003): 56.

3

Networks

This chapter provides a general overview of the concepts involved in developing a computer network within your library or school. Although a computer can, and sometimes still does, exist as a completely stand-alone system, cut off from any other computers, it's becoming quite rare. You might occasionally see stand-alone computers with library-specific programs (such as Accelerated Reader) or other software that's dedicated to a single program or use (such as an online catalog), but most computers are used for multiple functions. With the types of functionality that you want a computer to handle, most computers will fill more than a single role. By filling multiple roles, there's less chance that any single program will be unavailable to students because of limited access points. Furthermore, as Internet access is required for a greater number of purposes, it's ideal to have as many computers as possible with that access. This is especially true for teachers in their classrooms who want to send a quick e-mail to parents when they have a free moment.

Therefore, you'll probably have all of your library computers networked together as a group and likely with the entire school. It's more efficient to have all of the computers available to search the Web, databases, and online catalog, as well as to have the ability to store files on the network. There's also a savings in terms of allowing multiple computers to share peripherals, such as printers, scanners, and other devices. Furthermore, it makes it easier for updating and maintaining software. While this chapter only covers the basics—you really need an entire book to talk about networks—it provides you with a simple understanding of how all of this works, as well as resources for additional information.

As with many technology issues, the computer network is seldom something that you decide upon alone. It's usually part of a larger school network in order to simplify computer maintenance, cost, and use throughout the facility. Therefore, the first step in planning is simply to talk with other people.[1] Find out what the administration and technology staff has in terms of long-range plans, and incorporate this into the library's technology plan. Look into what others schools and districts in the area have done and how satisfied they've been with the results. This is a coordinated, expensive, and time-consuming effort.

Clear lines of responsibility are also important to ensure that repairs, maintenance, and troubleshooting are provided. There should be district-level tech people and a building-level tech person.[2] Ideally, a building-level tech person would be full-time, but in smaller schools this position could be filled by a librarian, teacher, administrator, a part-time person, or an external tech person who has limited hours and access. Most likely there may be some shared responsibilities between these people. The important point is that problems, whether resolved at the building level or not, should be shared with those at the district level so that a coordinated effort can be made.

Another major step is funding. What you want to do and what you can do might not be compatible. Will the school have the money to support the technology plan? Or will outside funding in the form of grants and donations from local businesses also be required? Major sources of revenue include district funds, fund raising, school-business partnerships, and government grants.

Finally, as always with technology, the target is constantly moving. What you're planning for now will someday change. The future could hold more than just a simple network of computers; it could be an entirely wireless network, thin clients, advanced Web-based services, and the continuation of smaller, faster, cheaper components.[3]

WHAT IS A NETWORK?

In the simplest terms, a network is merely a group of connected computers. This may be developed in many forms based on need and size. The most familiar is probably the *local area network* (LAN), which would consist of computers in your building. In a traditional wired network, the limiting factor is the length of cables that can be run. A *wide area network* (WAN) would cover a multibuilding facility, an even larger *campus network* would cover a college or university, and a *metropolitan network* would cover much of a city. On a smaller scale, many of you may already have a simpler *home network*.

In terms of equipment required to set up a network, the basics include a *server* (the computer managing the network), *cabling* (for a wired network), *workstations* (the computers that students, faculty, and staff will be using), and *network software* (special software that the server uses to make all of these connections work). Additionally, when a single point of contact controls so much, an *uninterruptible power supply* for the server is a good choice. An uninterruptible power supply is basically a battery backup so that if the main power is out, even for a few moments, the computers will continue to run. Finally, each workstation needs a network card. Ethernet, or wired, computers must have a *network interface card*, which allows the Ethernet cable to be plugged into the computer. Wireless networks require their own wireless network cards.

A network also requires a server, a main computer that controls functions between all of the other computers on the network. Be sure to get a larger hard drive, as much memory as you can afford, a leading processor, and a powerful 300-watt (or more) power supply. A server must be robust to handle all of the computers connecting to it.

The network software is referred to as the client/server *network operating system*. Some of the more well-known options include Novell Netware, Converging Technologies LANtastic, Microsoft Windows Server, and Windows NT. A centralized network would require different software for the thin client model, which we will look at later.

WIRED (ETHERNET)

The two main network categories are wired or wireless. Wired, the most common, has been around longer and is less expensive. Referred to as an *Ethernet*, it consists of physically connecting the server and computers with, most likely, long cables.

The topology of a wired network can come in many forms.[4] A *topology* is basically the way that the workstations are arranged geometrically and connected to each other and the server. The most common is called a star in which each workstation, known as a *node*, directly connects to a common *hub* (see figure 3.1). Thus, each workstation is independent of the others and, therefore, is more fault tolerant because a problem with one does not affect another. However, it can take a lot of cabling to connect every workstation. The larger the network—and, hence, the farther away from one another they have to be placed—the more cabling is required.

Other topologies include the bus and the ring. With a bus, a single cable acts as a backbone and all the computers attach to it, and with the ring, workstations are daisy-chained in a circular loop. The problem with the ring is like that of a chain, whereby it's only as strong as the weakest link. If

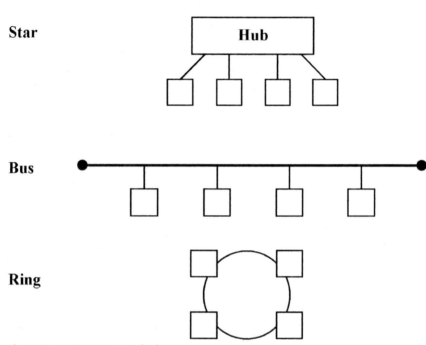

Figure 3.1.   Common Topologies

one computer fails, the entire network is disabled. Similarly, in a bus topology, a single break in the line will disrupt the entire network.

The benefit of this more mature wired technology is the speed. The *protocol* for the standard Ethernet is speeds up to 10 Mbps (megabits per second). Fast Ethernet (100Base-T) is up to 100 Mbps. Beyond that is Gigabit Ethernet with up to 1,000 Mbps. Most schools use the standard Ethernet protocol.

The *architecture* of the network includes the type of cabling that you will be using. The most common type of cable is *Category 5*, which has a maximum range of 100 meters and can transfer data at rates up to 100 Mbps. More powerful *Category 6* is used for Gigabit Ethernet, which is not as common in today's schools.

WIRELESS

Wired networks function by sending and receiving packets of information over cables, whereas wireless works by sending data via radio waves.[5] You can see the advantage of not having to worry about tripping over cables and to be able to easily rearrange and reconfigure space for equipment. However, wireless networks haven't been around as long as wired, tend to be a little slower and more expensive, and require a bit more planning. On the other hand, wireless technology is improving and is becoming much more competitive. There'll be a point in the near future when wireless overtakes wired as the predominant choice. In that case, the library will truly become the classroom and the classroom will become the library in terms of technology access.

Several different specifications make up the 802.11 series for wireless networks. This IEEE (Institute of Electrical and Electronics Engineers) specification dictates what can and can't be done. 802.11b has become popularized as Wireless Fidelity (*Wi-Fi*). It's not the fastest protocol, with top speeds of 11 Mbps, but it has a decent range of a few hundred feet. Therefore, fewer access points are required to be placed around the school. 802.11a is much faster at 54 Mbps, but it only has a range of about 60 feet, which makes it less practical for a large school. Instead, it would be ideal for a small home. 802.11g is more comparable to the wired Ethernet in terms of speed, and it also provides the range of 802.11b. 802.11n is now leading new installations so will take some time to become the new norm, with faster speeds up to 144 Mbps. The up-and-coming WiMax 802.16d for fixed and 802.16e for mobile appears to be the next step in this evolution, offering broadband speed of up to 70 Mbps at a much farther distance, up to 37 miles. This could potentially allow rural users to have broadband Internet access even if they are too remote for cable or DSL.

One of the concerns with networks is security. With wired networks, you still have to be concerned with firewalls, but wireless networks are even more difficult to control because the radio waves are traveling freely through the air. To circumvent others from tapping into that transmitted data, three elements are required for a wireless network: authentication, encryption, and data integrity.[6] *Wired Equivalent Privacy* (WEP) is a wireless security protocol that helps protect your information by using a security setting (called a WEP key) to encode, or encrypt, all network traffic before transmitting it over the airwaves. This helps prevent unauthorized users from accessing the data as it's being transmitted. Furthermore, WPA2 (Wi-Fi Protected Access 2) is the newer second generation of WPA security, providing enterprise and consumer Wi-Fi users with additional safety. Some users have also migrated to a more efficient *Temporal Key Integrity Protocol* and work is in progress to develop the next generation *Advanced Encryption Standard.*[7]

Another limitation of wireless networks is the varied range based on physical objects. Most rated distances for proper transmission of data only occur with a direct line of sight. Radio waves can be weakened by attenuation (damping), dispersion, reflection, and absorption.[8] Therefore, such objects as windows, wood doors, metal doors, and concrete walls can have a large impact on the actual range. Be prepared to add or move wireless ports to keep everything connected.

Wired is faster, cheaper, and more secure. However, wireless is more adaptable, improving, and coming down in price every day.

THIN CLIENTS

It's been said that those who forget the past are doomed to repeat it. That may very well be the case, but sometimes we want to go back. There are advantages to creating a thin network environment in your library media center and schools, which might sound strangely cyclical. Let's look at some history first.

Those of you who've been around a bit longer may remember the pre-PC days. Very large and very expensive mainframes handled all the processing, and users interacted with the system through dumb terminals, which were not much more than a monitor and keyboard.[9] Displays were limited to letters and numbers with fixed rows and columns. Although the interfaces were simplistic by today's standards, the advantage was having the ability to give multiple people access to a computer at the same time.

But this technology was still out of reach for most schools, and it wasn't until the development of the PC (the "fat client") in the early 1980s that we saw the first practical applications that we see in everyday schools. With the PC came circulation systems, online catalogs, e-mail, databases, websites, WebQuests, and much, much more. PC prices dropped, and what once required a large computer could be reproduced at a local level many times over: multiple computers could be purchased, entire labs could be outfitted, and PCs could be spread around the school. PCs improved continually and featured larger local hard drives, faster processors, multiple storage formats (5¼-inch disks, then 3½-inch disks, CD-ROM, DVD, CD-RW, etc.), sound, graphics, and video, all while becoming less expensive.

LANs, WANs, and the Internet allowed connectivity, communication, and shared resources. With programs and resources shared on the network, some of the burden could be lifted off the individual PCs. The next logical step in this age of interconnectedness was to let the server perform not just some but all of the work and replace the PCs with thin clients. Sounds like we've gone back to the mainframe.

In all fairness, it's not a simple choice. One of the main advantages of using thin clients is the cost savings. Each dumb terminal is roughly half the price of a PC because you don't need the hard drive, CD/DVD drive, and other components. However, you then need a very robust server with a lot of RAM (random-access memory), and there are licensing costs, so the final cost savings may not be as great as once expected. As PC prices continue to drop, the savings will be sliced even further.[10] Overall, *total cost of ownership* is lower for thin clients. PCs require a lot more maintenance, and this really does make them more expensive when employee time is factored in.

On the other hand, with a single server there's much less to do in terms of installing and maintaining software. You only have one computer to touch instead of many, and this saves a lot of time and money. Furthermore, as more and more resources are accessed via the Web and *application service providers* (ASPs) provide software entirely via a Web connection, there's less need to have that much power on the desktop. Thin clients work best where patrons do most of their work via a browser.[11] We can foresee the day when online catalogs will all be ASP driven just as our databases, full-text resources, and reference materials are subscriptions to websites. There's even talk that the common CD and DVD will disappear as music, movies, and software will all be transferred over the Internet on an as-needed basis. For example, many of you may have recently upgraded your antivirus software on your home computers by paying online for another year of service updates and then downloading the latest virus definitions. You don't need that physical disk any longer. Furthermore, students can even access those programs on the server, including CD-ROMs, from home.[12]

So why hasn't this taken off yet? When you have something so complex in place already, people are naturally reluctant to make radical changes. People also worry about having a single computer (server) responsible for so many others. Furthermore, during thin-client infancy there were problems with sharing CD-ROMs and also with printing.[13] Although these kinks have been worked out, familiarity with existing PCs and LANs makes a transition to a thin-client network sound expensive and daunting—even when the long-term benefits sound attractive.

The two main types of thin clients are *Network computer* (NC) and *Windows terminal* (WT). NCs include a processor, memory, monitor, mouse, and keyboard. Programs from the server are sent to the terminal and run locally and then saved to the server. Manufacturers of NCs include Sun Microsystems, IBM, Neoware, and Acorn Computers. WT networks, on the other hand, just send keystrokes. All of the work is done on the server.[14] The most well-known option is Citrix Metaframe, although there's also a free *Linux Terminal Server Project*.

Microsoft Windows NT Terminal Server uses the *Remote Desktop Protocol*. Citrix uses a more efficient *Independent Computing Architecture*. Citrix is considered a bit more robust but is also more expensive. HP's *Essential Series* can provide low-cost terminals for less than $200 each.[15]

While thin clients have a great number of advantages, shrinking prices have rapidly dissolved some of their attraction. With increased processing power of computers there are simple plug-in devices that can use a single

PC with connections for multiple monitors, keyboards, and mice, thereby allowing multiple simultaneous users. This reduces the total number of PCs that have to be purchased. Furthermore, as wireless networks become more common and laptop prices drop, the future may be a one-computer-per-child environment. This seems to be the most likely scenario, as *netbooks*, laptops with 7- to 10-inch screens, have become smaller, cheaper, lighter, and more powerful.

WEBSITES

About: Networking 101: http://compnetworking.about.com/od/basic networkingconcepts
Citrix: www.citrix.com
Converging Technologies: LANtastic: www.spartacom.com/products/lantastic.htm
Linux Terminal Server Project: www.ltsp.org
Microsoft: What is a network?: www.microsoft.com/windowsxp/using/networking/expert/bowman_02december16.mspx
Novell: www.novell.com
TechTutorials: Networking: www.techtutorials.net/tutorials/networking.html
Webopedia Local Area Network: www.webopedia.com/TERM/L/local_area _network_LAN.html
Webopedia Network: www.webopedia.com/TERM/N/network.html
Wi-Fi Alliance: www.wi-fi.org

NOTES

1. Miriam Barton, "Getting Wired: A School Computer Network," *LLA Bulletin* 61, no. 3 (Winter 1999): 184–87.

2. Becky Mather, *Creating a Local Area Network in the School Library Media Center* (Westport, CT: Greenwood, 1997), 90–91.

3. Joe Slowinski, "What Will the Future of Education Look Like?" *Book Report* 20, no. 4 (January/February 2002): 18–20.

4. Gilbert Held, *Ethernet Networks: Design, Implementation, Operation, Management* (New York: Wiley, 1998), 15.

5. Marshall Breeding, "A Hard Look at Wireless Networks," *Library Journal Net Connect* (Summer 2002): 14–17.

6. Joseph Davies, *Deploying Secure 802.11 Wireless Networks with Microsoft Windows* (Redmond, WA: Microsoft, 2004), 13.

7. William Cheswick, Steven Bellovin, and Aviel Rubin, *Firewalls and Internet Security: Repelling the Wily Hacker* (Boston: Addison-Wesley, 2003), 39–40.

8. Axel Sikora, *Wireless Personal and Local Area Networks* (West Sussex, England: Wiley, 2003), 29–30.

9. Mark Sheehan, "Thin Clients and Network-Centric Computing," *Online* 22, no. 6 (November/December 1998): 89–92.

10. Joe Huber, "Buzzing about New Technologies," *Book Report* 20, no. 4 (January/ February 2002): 50.

11. Joyce Latham, "Everything Old Is Thin Again," *School Library Journal Net Connect* (Fall 2001): 20–22.

12. Ross Gordon, "Thin Client Architecture in Libraries," *Feliciter* 47, no. 2 (2001): 78–80.

13. Walter Minkel, "Stretch Your Network," *School Library Journal* 48, no. 8 (August 2002): 52–53.

14. Susan Speer and Daniel Angelucci, "Extending the Reach of the Thin Client," *Computers in Libraries* 21, no. 3 (March 2001): 46–50.

15. Charles Babcock, "HP Upgrades Thin Clients in Wake of Windows 7," *InformationWeek* 2009, www.informationweek.com/news/software/hosted/showArticle .jhtml?articleID=222000355 (December 2, 2009).

2

INFORMATION RESOURCES

4

Educational Software

The second part of this book covers information resources that school librarians support electronically. This includes educational software, the Web in general, and the creation and maintenance of your own school library website. The library website and what students see when they sit down at the library computer becomes a library for them, especially when they're utilizing library resources from a classroom or from home.

Finding accurate, helpful information resources has always been a challenge, but it's become even more complicated. No longer are books and journals the only way of finding, sharing, and learning information. Information is now stored on a variety of media, both linear in nature and not, all of which can greatly supplement other library and classroom resources. Computer software has evolved into a myriad of options, and because of evolving hardware these options have become more and more complex.

Librarians are the experts to whom teachers, parents, and students look for help in accessing these resources, especially educational software. Some of these products may be housed in the library or a computer lab, strewn throughout the school, located on a server, accessed via the Web, or stored on home computers. Librarians, because of their skill in evaluating materials, knowledge of the curriculum throughout the entire school, and technical expertise, are naturals at providing resources for finding and evaluating software, passing on reviews, and determining if the purchase would be a good fit for the students.

Information literacy, by its very nature today, is tied to related concepts in computer literacy. On one hand, experience with computers and technology is an end in itself for students. It builds skills to be used throughout their lives and increases their comfort level in using these tools, which will lead to more complex activities as they progress. Teachers see educational software as a way to save time and pass some of the learning into another medium so that they can better distribute their own time, possibly with students who need additional one-on-one or small-group support. The software can also be viewed as a reward, something for students to strive for. This motivational factor might not have the same impact for every student, but it's a factor nonetheless. Finally, the software provides the educational support that might not be found in other resources and, due to the nature of the program, has benefits that serve the needs of various learning styles.

The names by which we call this software are varied. Some refer to it as *Computer-Assisted Instruction, Computer-Based Instruction,* or *Computer-Based Learning,* among other names. This is largely a matter of preference; in reality, the terminology used makes little difference. The different names do have different connotations, but everyday use has eliminated much of that distinction. What's important is that we recognize how the program fits into the curriculum, as opposed to simply having a game of some type that does little if any good.

As the technology has improved, so too has the complexity of the software. There are still vast differences between the products you can buy, so you have to keep the purpose in mind. Sometimes a simple review or drill program is all that's needed. Or sometimes you really do want the complex immersive program that could take the place of an entire teaching unit. Software today is seldom a couple floppy disks, as was the case in years back, but instead requires a CD-ROM, a DVD, or a Web browser (if it's entirely online). This means that hardware needs to be kept up-to-date in order to run these programs. You need to look at the product specifications to see if it includes a license for a single user or an entire site license for the school. Does running the program require the physical medium, such as a CD-ROM or DVD, or can you place it on the server for multiple users? Can students access the program from home or are you limited to the school site, a single lab, or that single computer?

Support for classroom technology may not end there because teachers might need help in installing, troubleshooting, and learning the software. They might also need advice on how to incorporate the software into their own units and how best to work the students into using the programs. Advice may also be provided regarding additional or related library resources to supplement the software program. Parents might also want to know more. Some students might need additional help on a specific area, and parents may ask for recommendations on what they can do. For instance, a parent might want to use a tutoring program at home to learn keyboarding skills. It could be something as simple as a math program for drilling the basics or as complex as a more immersive simulation. Regardless, just as parents once asked for opinions about encyclopedias and dictionaries for home use or specific book titles or series that would fit their child's reading level and interests, they're now asking about electronic resources, such as software and websites.

Educational software continues to evolve and mirror education in general. Just as the classroom was first seen from more of a behaviorist perspective, so, too, were the early software programs. Although there's still a time and place for behaviorist learning models, newer, and usually more expensive, programs are able to take on the look and feel of a constructivist learning environment. In this respect, "rather than passively responding to instructional stimuli imposed by a teacher, the learner generates his own meaning of what is experienced. Learning in this view is an active, constructive process which is based on existing knowledge and past experience."[1]

ISSUES

With any tool, its use involves positives and negatives. From the earliest tools to the most complicated technology available, people have worried about changing how things have always been done in the past. The basic concept behind educational software is that the computer takes the role of teacher. This can be a difficult concept for some to accept, and some will worry that use of computers means an inferior educational experience or one in which teachers are completely replaced. However, most of us realize that extremes are always dangerous. Computer software isn't a threat to teachers, but it won't solve all our problems either. Most realize that the concept of the computer as a tool with limited and specified use isn't true and that computers can instead enhance the traditional classroom. Librarians can help to support this role.

Let's take a closer look at some of the negatives. Some argue that these educational software programs aren't very educational and instead create a gaming or play-time environment. Quality does indeed vary, and some of the software available does purposely try to be fun and entertaining to keep the students' attention.

With the glitzy quality of some of these programs, some worry that any increases in student learning and motivation are only temporary as the novelty effect will wear off. Kids today are being bombarded by faster action, more special effects, and increased technology and graphics everywhere they turn. They're drawn to computer use in the school environment, but can it keep up? What about those students who've grown up with such software? Is it possible that some day down the road we'll see classes of students to whom none of this is new, and they'll complain that what they have in their possession is nothing more revolutionary than what has always existed to them? The bar keeps getting raised higher. A slick presentation with high-quality, content-rich programs requires an entire production team; a single person can't do it.

In addition, some programs tend to focus on relatively simple functions, such as drill and practice. It might seem that the processing power available is sometimes overkill for what students are being asked to do, and they aren't as excited about these programs as they once were.

Though these negatives exist, educational software—and software in general—has improved with the increase in memory and processor speed. This improvement is leading to new ways of using computers in the classroom. Computers are consistently being asked to do more and more. One of their key abilities is to tailor themselves to the individual. These more complex programs can adjust the difficulty level or the direction of the program based on student input, thereby providing an environment that's student specific. With large classrooms, it can be difficult for a teacher to provide that level of individualization, but a software program can adapt to user needs.

Because of the multimedia graphics and sounds in much educational software, different learning styles can be met. Howard Gardner's theories on multiple intelligences and other related learning theories point out that everyone has certain strengths, weaknesses, and preferences for learning.[2] Programs with varied interfaces and interactions are suited for working with all kinds of students. Many things simply can't be done otherwise. Sometimes a student needs to see how things interact and move, a concept that can't be understood by some students with a simple description or a still photo.

Software can also provide immediate feedback for students, so they don't have to wait to see if they understood a process correctly. Teachers only have so much time, and it can be minutes, hours, or days before students find out that they've made a mistake on assignments they turn in. However, computer programs can instantly tell students if they were correct or not and then provide an explanation of what they may have missed.

Finally, well-designed educational software is neutral. All students are treated equally, and the information they're provided should be unbiased.

RESEARCH

One of the biggest concerns about the use of educational software is whether students actually benefit. There's a large variation in quality among products available, and educators must determine which instructional strategies to use, as well as when and how to incorporate them. The fun and games aspect of many programs can sometimes easily outweigh learning. Overall, the end result for teachers is that the outcome be similar to other classroom activities.

In study after study, "typically the results have shown that students learn about the same amount of material through the computer as through conventional instruction."[3] All other factors aside, the use of technology usually results in about the same degree of learning. Related studies in the use of technology for learning from a distance have also resulted in what's known as the "no significant difference" phenomenon. This has implied that the technology used doesn't make as much of a difference for learning as the impact made by the teacher.

This isn't much of a surprise. There's been a great deal of hype regarding what educational software can purportedly do for the classroom, but similar hype was placed on other technologies that didn't have as big of an impact as once hoped. When the vinyl phonograph record was invented, visionaries imagined a future where classroom teachers could be largely replaced and students would listen to audio lessons created by experts. Radio education and instructional television and various other technologies were hoped to be the big breakthrough. In the end, like computers, they serve a place. There's a motivational factor to consider, and teachers are more efficient by being able to spend time on other tasks, but these technologies are only tools to be used as supplements and not replacements.

EARLY ADVANCES

The concepts behind today's educational software predate computers. Some of these include everything from interactivity to audio and visual learning to extrinsic motivation. Constructivists like Jean Piaget[4] and later Seymour Papert[5] studied the developmental stages of children and theorized about the different types of instruction that would best work for different ages. Papert believed that between the ages of 8 and 14, children enter a concrete operational stage in which concrete examples (the ability to visually see the product) are important for understanding and, hence, learning.

Papert is best known for his work on LOGO. In its various forms, LOGO is an interactive learning system that allows children to learn from experience and uses logic and problem-solving techniques. The system is simple to learn, yet complex enough that students can grow and develop with it, creating ever-more complex results as they delve into the details.

The turtle is the icon that most people recognize from LOGO. The first LOGO system—developed before the personal computer—was a robotic "turtle" that students could program, nicknamed "the turtle," partially because of its appearance and partly because it moved slowly. Once placed on a floor covered by paper, the turtle would run the program the child created and move about on the floor, dragging a pen behind it. In this way, a final product of a geometric shape or picture would be drawn. It required that the user follow specific directions and steps to create the commands. It required logic and problem solving to determine which direction to turn, how far to move, and when to put the pen down or lift it up.

Although cumbersome, the turtle was both fun and educational. With the development of computers, the same concept was easily translated into an easier-to-use program. The mechanical turtle became the turtle cursor on the computer screen, and students could easily program the turtle and then watch it carry out the instructions. It was now even easier for students to create ever-more complex patterns and run through the steps at the push of a button.

LOGO has kept up with changes in technology with their Microworlds products. Although even more complex, the basic principle is still the same: allow the student to enter a world where the learning environment is open-ended. There's no direct path for a student to follow like a story reads from start to finish. Instead, the tools are made available with parameters for students to follow, and then they let their imaginations and ingenuity flow.

TYPES OF EDUCATIONAL SOFTWARE

Educational software can be divided into many different categories based on its purpose and method of instruction. Although the lines can sometimes be blurred and some programs can include a variety of different categories, we need to understand these categories to better determine where and when they should be used.

Concept Processing

Concept-processing programs fall along the lines of productivity software. These programs easily allow the user, whether an individual or a group, to brainstorm ideas or organize thoughts. While this can be done via paper or on a word processor in the form of a text outline or a colorful artistic drawing, this software makes it easy to erase, change, and move items around. The graphical nature and easy-to-modify environment create an open-ended place for students to collect thoughts and ideas, which can then be used for other activities. Popular products include Inspiration and Kidspiration.

Drill and Practice

Drill and practice programs dominated the early days of educational software. The simplest programs are little more than electronic flash cards. However, even flash cards have their place, and sometimes students need additional practice. More advanced software will change with the user's development, allowing the difficulty level to automatically adjust based on the error rate. In this way, all students are challenged at the appropriate level.

Because of their drill-and-practice nature, these programs require that the student understand the concepts ahead of time. The program isn't meant to teach the user how to solve the problems, but simply to test them. Therefore, concepts must be taught by the teacher, self-taught, or learned through books and other media.

In addition, there's seldom instruction on how to fix mistakes. Students are told what's wrong and what's right, providing immediate feedback—one of the main benefits of these programs—however, the programs seldom explain why it was wrong or how to do it better the next time. It's merely a way for students who already know the concepts to get extra practice.

Tutorial

In contrast to drill-and-practice programs, tutorials teach the student how to do something. In the early days, tutorials were simplistic, comprising little more than electronic page turners. The content was similar to what could alternatively be found in printed material but with a few extra bells and whistles. Students learned by following along and reading.

Today's faster computers and larger storage devices allow a greater deal of complexity. Although these tutorials can still be linear in nature like a book or have linear sections, branching off into new lessons based on student interest or decisions allows for a much more fluid environment and one that approaches what interaction with a teacher can do on the fly. Therefore, entire lessons can be given to students that provide feedback and interactivity, completely explaining the entire subject in one place.

Simulation

Simulations allow the student to become part of the instruction and visualize the learning environment as if they're part of it. Whether this environment is based on a real-world situation or is entirely imaginary, the learner can see a perspective that otherwise wouldn't be available. This might be a place that they simply couldn't travel to, or it might demonstrate something that couldn't easily be done in the real world. In another sense, this control over the environment gives the learner a control over their own direction that usually isn't permitted otherwise. There are several different types of simulations: those that teach about something and those that teach how to do something. The four main types of simulations are physical, iterative, procedural, and situational.[6] Physical simulations are those in which the learner manipulates objects, such as computerized chemistry or physics experiments. Iterative simulations allow the learner to speed up or slow down processes in a manner that would otherwise be difficult to understand. These could include speeding up geologic processes to see change over long periods of time or slowing down movements of particles to see how they interact. Procedural simulations teach the learner the proper sequence of steps required for success in an environment that they otherwise wouldn't have access to (e.g., flight simulator programs). Finally, situational simulations provide the learner with a hypothetical situation and then ask the student to find a solution (e.g., playing the stock market).

Simulations have been around since the 1950s as a component of military training.[7] Their popularity in schools peaked, waned, and came back into the spotlight again as processing power and realism have generated a new generation of applications. While the traditional lecture is often noted as being more effective in transmitting factual knowledge, simulations provide complex models and situations that are difficult to envision any other way.

Instructional Games

Instructional games, like many of the other types of software, can be difficult to define because they tend to blend together and provide multiple components. The main objective in these games is still to provide some type of educational aspect, but it's more or less overshadowed by highly motivational play. This often includes extensive multimedia features, such as graphics and sound.

A vast majority of these games focus on drill and practice or on simulation software intertwined with game rules. Winning the game is usually the objective for the child, with learning more of a by-product. Some educators fear that learning is marginalized and that these programs aren't worth the time. Others argue that it doesn't hurt to use games to reinforce a specific lesson; the message is still getting across. Games can also be used as a reward mechanism or a break from other activities.

Others believe that in order to compete with the gaming opportunities children have at home, some type of similar activity must be placed into lessons. "Games teach children what computers are beginning to teach adults—that some forms of learning are fast-paced, immensely compelling, and rewarding. . . . Not surprisingly, by comparison, school strikes many young people as slow, boring, and frankly out of touch."[8] In this respect, we find ourselves in competition for student attention. That doesn't necessarily mean that all learning goes out the door, but it does mean that there should be room for multiple activities and approaches.

Problem Solving

Problem-solving activities can be among the most challenging for some students because they involve more than just finding the answer or following a simple set of procedures. Teachers can spend a lot of time preparing these activities and working with students. By using software that's more complex in order to reach that higher-order learning, teachers free themselves to work with students who need more guidance. Problem-solving activities can include puzzles, riddles, and mysteries. Instead of teaching new concepts and information, these activities are intended to give students practice figuring out how to solve the problems they're presented with. Whether completed individually or in a small group around the computer, these activities can create discussion and complex thinking.

In a related manner, students can use the library itself as a way to solve problems. Searching the library for answers isn't a strict linear procedure with an answer at the end but a more complex series of steps and evaluations along the way, branching out as new information is found.

Integrated Learning Systems

Integrated learning systems are basically a combination of the different types of educational software available. The key is that the software maker has created a turnkey integrated system in which an entire series of offerings is packaged together into a single product that provides one-stop shopping. The integrated system may span different age ranges or topics, but the goal is to provide something that includes multiple modules. The benefit is a more cohesive approach, one that might be less expensive overall because you're basically buying in bulk.

Intelligent Tutoring Systems

Intelligent tutoring systems take tutorials one step further. They provide expert knowledge, learner modeling, planning, and communication to provide an experience for the student that resembles as closely as possible one that could be provided by a teacher.[9] The difference between these advanced systems and all others lies in their constructivist approach, as compared to the older behaviorist models of learning.

Educational software spans a continuum, with programs ranging from linear computer-assisted instruction, to more complex branching computer-assisted instruction, to elementary intelligent computer-assisted instruction, to entirely autonomous or stand-alone intelligent computer-assisted instruction.[10] The intention is that for these specific purposes, the computer system can replace the teacher. The continuum, therefore, seems to represent a worse-to-better progression, simple to more complex, partial to complete. However, as with everything else, the software's use must still be considered within the larger context of the classroom. At specific times, these intelligent systems indeed are very useful. The environment is complex, and teachers and librarians still need to determine when and how that the software fits into the entire lesson unit.

Reference

Reference software are those information resources that students will find useful whether in the library, in the classroom, or at home. They can range from encyclopedias to dictionaries to very subject-specific reference sources. These collections of resources are ever-more important as students find themselves inundated with larger and larger amounts of information. A student can waste a lot of time hunting down information on the Web and then trying to determine if the information is accurate, when only a simple encyclopedia entry was needed.

EVALUATING EDUCATIONAL SOFTWARE

Selection and acquisition of materials has become more complicated with ever-increasing formats and as materials may potentially be used outside of the physical library. The school librarian plays an important role when selecting and acquiring books for use in the library and throughout the school. These include fiction, nonfiction, biographies, and also professional development materials for teachers. This now includes software titles as well. These can be used within the library, in a library computer lab or another nearby lab, or directly in the classroom. Depending on the individual school, the librarian most likely works in concert with teachers to review and evaluate these titles, matching them to specific curricular needs, similar to determining what books are needed. However, with expanded software use throughout classrooms, the teacher may be the one that uses the materials more on a day-to-day basis, and the librarian becomes more of a guide. This is where the librarian's expertise in evaluating materials, managing materials budgets, and working with vendors comes into play.

Why is the evaluation process important? Partially it's important because of the costs involved. Software programs tend to cost more than a single book, and the more complex ones can truly be expensive. Evaluation is important to avoid spending a large amount of money on an item that gets little or no use. Furthermore, the evaluation process creates an opportunity for the librarian and teacher to communicate about student needs, and it can grow into discussions about curricular needs and other chances for using resources and collaboration.

How can materials be reviewed? As a contact person, the teacher or librarian may come across software titles from various places: reviews in professional literature, ads in other journals, observation at other schools, or discussion with other teachers and librarians. Most vendors will let you install and run the program for a limited trial period at no cost. Some vendors are a bit more cautious and will only allow a software demo. Although useful, the demos are usually fairly limited in functionality yet will often provide a good idea of how useful it could be. The software can often be downloaded directly from a website or from a CD received via mail on request.

The process of evaluating software includes first finding the software. This can be done by coming across a title and deciding that it fills a need or, instead, by determining that there's a need and then hunting down what software programs are available. Possible sources of titles include catalog listings from publishers, professional journals, popular journals, professional meetings, and other teachers.[11]

Once an item is found, a preview or demo is requested, downloaded, and installed on a single computer. Librarian and teachers then have the opportunity to review the software and determine if it's something that they'd like to pursue. The actual budgeting process will vary from school to school, but the librarian should be involved and know if money is available (whether in charge of that line or not) and then order the software when administrative approval is given and the budget allows.

The review process should be documented and taken seriously (see figure 4.1). Some areas that must be considered are accuracy of information, appropriateness, bias, quality, ease of use, learner control, feedback, motivation, interaction, graphics and audio, documentation, help features, record keeping, report generation, and cost. By going through a checklist to thoroughly evaluate a program, the teachers and librarians will be sure to take the time to think about everything and not be distracted by a glitzy interface or a few points that overshadow the whole. It also gives everyone involved a chance to compare their notes afterward to ensure that something wasn't missed. Then each person can go back and look at any issues. This will help to ensure that money and time aren't wasted on poor purchases.

Software title_____

Publisher_____

Website_____ Phone_____

Pricing per license and/or total cost_____

Where the software was heard about_____

Format (circle):　　　　CD　　DVD　　Networked　　Web Based

Operating system_____

RAM_____

Processor_____

Other equipment required (speakers, microphone, Internet access)_____

_____

Number of simultaneous users_____

Content area_____

Grade level(s)_____

Rate each criterion below from 1 (low) to 5 (high) or not applicable/not found (n/a)

1. Instructional Design

___Instructional level is appropriate for the stated audience

___Learner is involved in a high degree of interaction

___Appropriate feedback is provided

___Problem solving and the development of higher order thinking skills are promoted

___Software is adaptable to a variety of teacher and learning styles

___Programs contain multiple levels of difficulty

___Responses to the learner are not highly repetitive

2. Presentation Design

___Instructions are clear, concise, and complete

___Simple commands allow the learner to navigate throughout the program

___Teacher or the learner determines the pace at which the user moves through the
program

___Learner can alter responses before they are processed

___User interface is consistent

___Users at all levels can easily and independently operate the program

___Help screens provide clear, understandable explanations for all aspects of the
program

___Audio and visuals are high quality

___User can save and/or print work in progress

___Appropriate use is made of motion or live action sequences and still images

___Sound can be controlled by the teacher or the learner

3. Ease of Use

___New users can easily learn how to use the program

___Students have access to materials and concepts not possible with traditional print
formats

___Information on the screen indicates where the student is in the program

___Backtracking one step at a time is simple

___Results, if applicable, can be saved
___Printing of relevant information is available
___Visual/graphical icons or images are used
___Results can be downloaded into and manipulated with other programs
___Print request informs the user of the total number of page before printing
___Estimate of time needed for classroom use is given
___Suggested activities are consistent in quality and tone
___Appropriate teacher support materials are available

4. Content

___No grammar, spelling, or punctuation errors
___Up-to-date and accurate
___No cultural, gender, or racial bias
___Utilizes examples that encourage students to explore roles they may not have considered
___Stimulates critical thinking and problem-solving activities
___Stimulates curiosity and creative activities
___Supports cooperative group work
___Appropriate to student needs, curriculum area, purpose, and grade level
___Supports one or more instructional goals

5. Motivation

___Provides for various learning modalities (e.g., auditory, kinesthetic, and/or visual)
___Provides an intellectual challenge and/or encourages creativity on the part of the learner

6. Technical Quality

___Program does not break no matter what the student does
___High-quality stereo reproduction and sound separation is included
___Motion sequences flow smoothly on recommended hardware
___Program installation requires minimal level of computer expertise
___Staff time for maintenance is reasonable
___Versions are available for multiple operating systems
___Help functions are easy to follow
___800 number is provided for assistance at no cost

Comments:

_____
_____
_____

_____
___Recommended   ___Not recommended
Evaluator's rating: On a scale of 1 to 5, with 5 being the highest_____
Evaluator:_____ Date:_____

Figure 4.1.   Software Evaluation Form

IMPLEMENTATION AND SUPPORT

Schools vary in terms of personnel structure, with some having a librarian as a technology coordinator and others having a technology coordinator as a completely different position. Some school districts have district technology coordinators who move from school to school throughout the week. In that case, there might be a need for a local technology coordinator who oversees day-to-day and limited technology issues. That's a great place for a school librarian.

Whether the librarian or someone else installs the actual software, the librarian is more likely to be nearby and available to help troubleshoot any problems—especially if he or she has a flexible schedule. Furthermore, librarians are more likely to understand how the software program actually works and should be used, beyond the nuts and bolts of installing and setting up. By working with the classroom teacher, the librarian can also help to incorporate the software into the curriculum, with other resources, and within unit lesson plans.

WEBSITES

Children's Technology Review: www.childrenssoftware.com/

Discovery School: http://school.discovery.com/parents/reviewcorner/ software

Evalutech: www.evalutech.sreb.org

Inspiration: www.inspiration.com

Logo Foundation: http://el.media.mit.edu/logo-foundation

The No Significant Difference Phenomenon website: www.nosignificant difference.org

PC Magazine: www.pcmag.com

SuperKids Educational Software Review: www.superkids.com

TechLEARNING: http://techlearning.com

NOTES

1. Paul Saettler, *Evolution of American Educational Technology* (Englewood, CO: Libraries Unlimited, 1990), 478.

2. Howard Gardner, *Frames of Mind: The Theory of Multiple Intelligences* (New York: Basic Books, 1993).

3. Saettler, *Evolution of American Educational Technology*, 489.

4. Jean Piaget, *The Essential Piaget*, ed. Howard E. Gruber and J. Jacques Vonèche (New York: Basic Books, 1977).

5. Seymour Papert, *The Children's Machine: Rethinking School in the Age of the Computer* (New York: Basic Books, 1993).

6. M. D. Roblyer, *Integrating Educational Technology into Teaching* (Upper Saddle River, NJ: Pearson Education, 2003), 94.

7. Valerie J. Shute and Joseph Psotka, "Intelligent Tutoring Systems: Past, Present, and Future," in *Handbook of Research for Educational Communications and Technology*, ed. David H. Jonassen (New York: Macmillan, 1996), 521.

8. Papert, *The Children's Machine*, 5.

9. Saettler, *Evolution of American Educational Technology*, 537.

10. Shute and Psotka, "Intelligent Tutoring Systems," 570.

11. Paul G. Geisert and Mynga K. Futrell, *Teachers, Computers, and Curriculum: Microcomputers in the Classroom* (Needham Heights, MA: Pearson Education, 2000), 268–69.

5

The Internet

The Internet is a large topic because it can be described and used from so many different angles. School librarians know all too well about the difficulty of getting teachers, administrators, students, and parents to realize that everything isn't really available for free on the Web. The Internet is a resource for both communication and information, which the librarian is best trained to use. It's our job to educate others on finding and using these resources. However, this target is constantly moving. The Internet has evolved quickly over the past decade, and it takes continual effort to keep up with new developments and nuances. To further complicate the matter, students have different expectations, interests, and biases that can be difficult to handle. We have, on the one hand, tech-savvy students who know more than many of their teachers and, on the other hand, students who don't have the money for home computers and therefore require technology in the school to catch up. Trying to work with both extremes as well as those in the middle can be difficult from a planning perspective.

This chapter presents some background on how the Internet came to be in its present form. This is followed by information on the use of the Internet as both a communication and information tool. To approach using these resources from an information literacy perspective, we'll look at how to evaluate websites in general as well as how to approach educational websites. Finally, we'll look at some of the ways that we can incorporate Internet resources in the classroom by using WebQuests and virtual field trips.

BACKGROUND

It's hard to believe how quickly technology has changed. Recent advances in technology are but a blink of an eye in terms of human development. On the other hand, it's hard for most of us to even remember what it was like before we had the Internet. It's become so ingrained in our daily lives and taken for granted that it feels like it's always been there, and it's difficult to imagine what we would do without it.

Although the Web as we know it has only been around a little more than a decade, the necessary technological advancements needed as the precursor started much earlier. Without going back to rudimentary mathematics and other basic disciplines, one of the first truly related steps may have been in 1822 when Charles Babbage developed the first computing machine.[1] His *Difference Engine* was an attempt at the earliest concept of programming, performing only basic mathematical calculations. Simply based on a mechanical nature with rudimentary components, it laid the groundwork for future computers.

In conjunction with computer power, we also needed advances in communication across distances. In 1844, Samuel Morse invented the telegraph, ushering in the beginning of instant messaging. Related achievements, such as the first transatlantic cable in 1866 and Alexander Graham Bell's patent for the telephone in 1876, brought in concepts of a worldwide connection between people.

Early computers were large and expensive, filling entire rooms. The first step toward miniaturization and our seemingly constant need for faster, smaller, and cheaper computers started in 1947 when the simple transistor replaced large and fragile vacuum tubes.

ARPA, the Advanced Research Projects Agency, was created in 1958 in response to Russia's Sputnik the year prior. This is where the Internet would later be born. At this point, advances were coming along at much faster paces. In 1962, Paul Baran wrote a paper titled "On Distributed Communication Networks," a concept now known as packet switching.[2] Packet switching is one of the basic principles behind today's Internet, allowing computers to send information from one location to the next by breaking the message down into chunks, sending those chunks out along the shortest and/or fastest route, and then reassembling them at the other end. Before the Internet was even realized, people were theorizing what could be done if only technology could catch up with their imagination. In 1965, Ted Nelson, a pioneer in user interface design, introduced the terms *hypertext* and *hyperlink* for a then-theoretical computerized information system. It would take many more years before a practical application could be developed.

Finally, in 1969, four computers were connected together to form the ARPANET (Advanced Research Projects Agency Network), the very beginnings of the Internet. The universities of Utah, UCLA, UC Santa Barbara, and Stanford successfully sent information between their computers. The theoretical packet switching in which files were broken down into smaller chunks to be transmitted, and even rerouted to different paths if need be, was realized. This was the fledgling Internet. Although much more complicated, the Internet essentially is "a set of linked computers world-wide."[3]

In 1972, the "@" sign was chosen for e-mail addresses, a symbol that everyone today is familiar with and automatically relates to e-mail. But to realize the true development of a connected world, home computers still needed to be widespread, easy to afford, and simple to use. These beginnings finally came about in 1975 when the Altair 8800, the first microcomputer, was sold. At first, these computer kits were snatched up by computer enthusiasts and reflected the science fiction flavor of the technology—the computer was named after a fictional planet from the original, and at that time the only, *Start Trek* TV series. From the start, however, consumers were bombarded by continual replacement cycles as computers kept improving at steady rates.

Although these early computers were driven by command line interfaces, cheat sheets, short cuts, and keyboard cards were seen as a small price to pay for the improved work flow. By 1984, these would start to be replaced by a GUI (Graphical User Interface) in Apple Macintosh computers. Shortly thereafter, in 1985, Microsoft developed the similar Windows interface that the public needed to become more attached to their computers and ease computer use. Graphical abilities continued to grow as processing power increased the options that programmers had access to.

Until this point, the Internet wasn't used by the general public. There was some e-mail, transferring of files, and a text-driven interface that didn't have any type of search engine. This changed in 1990 when independent contractors Tim Berners-Lee and Robert Cailliau proposed to CERN (European Organization for Nuclear Research, the world's largest laboratory for particle physics) the development of a hypertext system, the World Wide Web. Just as the command-driven days of the computer were being replaced by a windows environment, so too was the Internet. However, this was still theoretical and standards needed to be written.

In the meantime, other advances were taking place. In 1991, the University of Minnesota developed its Gopher, the first command-driven, yet easy way to access Internet sites. Shortly thereafter, in 1992, the University of Nevada developed Veronica, allowing users to perform advanced searches of Gopher servers, otherwise known as what's now called an "indexing spider."[4]

During this same time span, around 1991, Berners-Lee and a team at CERN developed the building blocks of the Web: HTTP (hypertext transfer protocol), HTML (hypertext markup language), and the URL (universal resource locator). With those in place, 1993 saw the birth of the first graphical browser, Mosaic. The Web was here and there was no going back. Since then, there has been a flurry of new developments, with Ajax, Java, HTML5, and other ways of making the Web more interactive, flashy, and easier to use.

The Web (World Wide Web or WWW) is really just an interface to one component of the Internet.[5] It provides a structure for finding and retrieving "hypertext documents" in which one document will link you to another graphically. The Web is based on a client/server architecture.[6] In this respect, client programs can be seen as Web browsers that simply connect to the Web servers around the world. These browsers and servers follow a specific set of rules or protocols, including HTTP, FTP (file transfer protocol), Gopher, telnet, and many others.

Although the Web might seem to be the dominate way of accessing the Internet, many of the underlying structures are still present. Gophers, while not really used any longer, are just command-driven interfaces for accessing textual files as opposed to the graphical files of the Web. Telnet can still be used to connect to and log into remote computers. Largely done today with a graphical Web interface, the concept is the same. Finally, you can still find text-based Web browsers that harken back to the old days. These browsers, such as Lynx, are suited now for people who have vision problems and don't need the graphics because they'll be using screen readers or simply for people who want a faster connection and don't want images.

To provide standardization in Web addresses, the Domain Name System was developed. Administered by Network Solutions, Inc. and the Internet Corporation for Assigned Names and Numbers (ICANN), this system consists of a specified set of domain names, the suffixes at the end of a root URL. Network Solutions, Inc. and ICANN also oversee the choice and use of possible future additions. For the present, these are the most common, and students should be aware of what they mean:

.com (commercial business and for-profit organizations)
.edu (four-year higher education)
.org (nonprofit organizations)
.gov (U.S. government)
.net (networking organizations)
.mil (U.S. military)
.int (international)
.post (postal offices)
.travel
.biz
.info
.museum

COMMUNICATION TOOL

The first and oldest primary use of the Internet is communication with other people. The second is as an information tool, a way of storing and retrieving information. Most of this communication has been done asynchronously, meaning that it takes place at different times and different places for different people. Communication is initiated, sent, stored, and then accessed later. This is similar to writing a letter and sending it through standard postal mail. There's a time lag between sending a message and receiving a reply. However, electronically the message is nearly instantaneous. The main reason for any type of wait is that people aren't on their computers at the same time.

The oldest and most widely used feature of the Internet is electronic mail, which we all know as e-mail—"an electronic mailbox . . . that will store messages until the user requests delivery."[7] School librarians use e-mail on a daily basis to communicate with other librarians, teachers, parents, and others. With the rise of Internet use at home and oftentimes the ability to check school e-mail accounts from any Internet connection, librarians are almost always in touch with anyone around the world.

Although school policies vary, student use of e-mail has also expanded rapidly. Often students will use their parents' e-mail addresses from home, or older students will have their own. At school, safety concerns or just plain mischief means that e-mail access has to be curtailed or monitored closely. With the ubiquitous nature of the evolving Internet and rising technical skills of students, it seems that these hurdles may eventually disappear. Although precise statistics have been difficult to find, student school e-mail accounts given to third and fourth graders are not unusual. However, this requires coordination to teach students safety and etiquette rules and for password distribution. Librarians are often involved in this process.

E-mail in school is a way for students to communicate with experts around the world, with distant students as a modern pen pal forum, with peers at a neighboring school, with the school administrators, and with teachers in a correspondence education course. Geography is no longer a limit, and online learning communities are growing in number. E-mail between classrooms in Russia and the United States started in 1998, and now the International Education and Resource Network has grown to more than 20,000 schools in over 100 countries. Some of this collaboration includes magazines, written anthologies, websites, reports to government officials, and creative performances.[8]

Other types of asynchronous communication tools include e-mail lists. These are mailing lists in which one person can send a message to everyone who has subscribed to the list. An open and unmoderated list can become dangerous for students, but with a moderator who ensures safety from spam and predators and with a teacher involved, e-mail lists on relevant topics can result in profitable communication. Librarians, who because of their work environment often have little if any daily contact with other library professionals, tend to be avid participants on electronic mailing lists. This is where an e-mail list can become very important for asking questions, sharing experiences, and working with others with the same issues. Electronic mailing lists like LM_NET are indispensable.

Another environment for students to share asynchronously with librarians, teachers, and each other is in discussion boards. Similar in concept to the e-mail list, discussion boards use software to organize and save the messages posted so that users can easily go back and revisit messages at their own convenience. Stand-alone software packages can be used or they can be bundled into larger course management software, such as Blackboard, Moodle, or eCollege.

The most common form of synchronous communication, conversing at the same time, is instant messaging (IM). Although audio conferencing via computer, which is similar to using a telephone, and video conferencing are becoming more prevalent with the use of microphones, Webcams, and fast Internet connections, there's still a lot of progress to be made in terms of ease of use, cost, and especially quality of transmission. Therefore, text-based IM is still prevalent. Because this type of communication can be disruptive in a classroom and difficult to monitor, it's usually not permitted, except for certain instances where the discussion has been planned ahead of time with a known user. IM software can be found free on the Web or bought as either stand-alone or packaged within a larger course-management system.

Conversing with other students, teachers, or experts via the Internet also provides a medium for sharing files in order to communicate. This can be done within e-mail and discussion boards, but it can also be done in other ways as well. Two of the standard means of sharing access to a file are via Telnet and FTP. Telnet is a protocol in which the user logs in to a computer from a remote site and directly accesses those resources as if he or she were a local user. Most of this is done today via a Web interface. FTP (file transfer protocol) is a way for people to send and retrieve files from remote locations. This, too, is often built into websites and especially Web editors as a way of publishing Web pages to a file server but can also be used to share large files with other users.

Blogs, Wikis, and other Web 2.0 tools have increasingly enhanced communication between and among students, teachers, and classrooms. A blog is a electronic Web version of a traditional paper journal. The author logs in and writes an entry that is available for others to read. Besides text, a blog entry could also include images and even sound and video clips. Students may keep this electronic journal as they work on a project or read a book, or teachers and librarians could use it as a way to share information with their students.

A wiki is a website that visitors can edit without having to use a Web editor. It is usually simple enough that the visitor clicks an edit button on the Web page, makes changes to the page, and then clicks a save button. With this truly collaborative tool, students can work on a project without being in the same room at the same time.

Online office suites, such as Google Docs, Zoho, and Microsoft Office, complete this area with the ability for students to collaborate and communicate at a distance with a Web-based application that works just like a word processor, spreadsheet, or presentation application. The benefit with this type of communication is that the final product is in the form that most teachers and librarians are already looking for.

INFORMATION TOOL

The Web is also an information tool, something that libraries have always promoted. However, librarians have to consider resources on the Web that they have to pay for, such as subscription databases and paid access to Websites, as well as information that is freely available.

Databases

It's hard to imagine school libraries without access to subscription databases. Although their use might not be as frequent or intensive in the lower grade levels, their widespread adoption is growing. Many states provide databases to public libraries and public schools for little or no cost. This is meant to level the playing field and save money by getting a large-group discount. Although this may only cover some very basic databases, it's certainly a start and then schools can decide what additional resources to add on their own.

Many people in the general public, and even some educators, think that anything one needs can be found on the Web for free. This mistaken thinking doesn't take into account the quality of materials and the fact that you often get what you pay for. Subscription databases provide quality resources that are accurate and timely.

A growing number of companies are providing niche services to supplement journal databases and standard websites. Some of these, such as BrainPop and United Streaming, offer short videos or video clips that can be used for classroom instruction. Either as short stand-alone informational pieces to start off a discussion or as a way to help students visualize what they're reading or learning about in class, these databases of videos provide a collection of resources that can't be found for free on the Web.

Nondatabase Subscriptions

Although access to paid-subscription databases often provides the highest authority for quality and content, there's also a growing field of website subscriptions that fill certain niches. This is starting to blend as companies are offering collections of video clips, image archives, sound files, encyclopedic resources, and content that serve specific needs not found elsewhere.

Usually less expansive compared to the large database vendors, these subscription websites may serve a specific class, an entire grade level, a subject area, or the entire school. Streaming video is one such service that's a very useful resource to supplement lessons. It's best to preview and evaluate these resources before subscribing, and be sure that the teachers involved will want to incorporate the content.

Websites

What's left after this are general websites that are freely available for people to use. Students and teachers most unfamiliar with library resources gravitate to these sites because they think that a Google search will meet their needs. While there's certainly a time and place for using general websites and wonderful resources are available, the hard part is trying to separate the good from the bad, especially as the number of websites continues to grow every year (see table 5.1 for a list of popular search engines).

One of the problems with textbooks in the classrooms is that they become out of date rather quickly. Access to the Internet provides up-to-date primary sources and expert information from around the world. Furthermore, students can gain international perspectives by, for example, accessing newspapers and other resources from other countries.[9]

The librarian's job in this respect is twofold. First, the librarian needs to be able to provide teachers and students with information on quality web-

Table 5.1.   Popular Search Engines

Search Engine	URL
Ask for Kids	www.askkids.com
bing	www.bing.com
dmoz	www.dmoz.org
dmoz for kids	www.dmoz.org/Kids_and_Teens
Google	www.google.com
KidsClick	www.kidsclick.org
KidsKonnect	www.kidskonnect.com
Yahoo	www.yahoo.com
Yahooligans	http://kids.yahoo.com

sites to supplement library resources. Second, the librarian needs to be able to teach others about finding and evaluating websites on their own.

EVALUATING WEBSITES

Evaluating websites is now common practice. School librarians need to be able to evaluate websites to find resources for students and teachers, to collaborate on lessons, and to provide subject links on the library website. Just as librarians are experts in evaluating books, videos, and software programs, they also need to be able to evaluate websites and teach others how to do so. This is the difficult part because many teachers and students have an inaccurate view of their skills. Many think that they can quickly type a search into Google and then pick out a couple sites from the thousands of hits. This is where the expertise of the librarian is important. Reinforcing good searching behavior is important and requires continued emphasis year to year as students mature. Figure 5.1 shows a sample of the type of evaluation form that a librarian might use after looking at a website.

The first things to look at when evaluating a website are the author and the purpose of the site. A site that's produced by a professional organization is more likely to be accurate than a commercial or personal site. A site that's authored by an expert in the field is more likely to be accurate than one written by your next-door neighbor. Whatever the purpose, it should be clear and easy to find.

A good website should also be current and up-to-date. Although facts on a historical site might not need any revisions, most information does because it's time sensitive. Similar to time-sensitive areas in your print resources, websites covering certain subject areas should be monitored more closely than others. At the very least, an updated site shows that some serious effort has been put into it since someone feels it's important to maintain.

Objectivity is crucial when determining whether the information provided is accurate. Bias can be found in many other forms of media also, but students can be easily distracted by an impressive-looking design. Appearances can mask the content, and students often gravitate toward those that look like more time and money has been spent on the site even though another simpler site might have better content.

The content of the site is what the entire purpose of using the resource is all about. Research is about finding multiple resources that can reinforce the findings the student is looking for. Therefore, more than a single website needs to be used in order to maintain that the information found is accurate. A good website will refer visitors to other websites and additional resources as references or support information.

Website Name:
Website URL:
Date Accessed:
Authority
    Information about the author provided   Yes   No
    Contact information for the author provided   Yes   No
    Purpose of the site clearly explained   Yes   No
    Domain of the website identifiable   Yes   No
Currency
    Updated recently   Yes   No
    No broken links   Yes   No
Objectivity
    Bias eliminated or at least clearly identifiable   Yes   No
    Authors' personal opinions do not affect the information provided   Yes   No
Content
    Information complements other resources in terms of accuracy   Yes   No
    Information detailed enough for given audience   Yes   No
    Information free from spelling and grammar errors   Yes   No
Design
    Overall appearance attractive and interesting   Yes   No
    Layout aesthetically pleasing with good use of white space   Yes   No
    Navigation easy to follow and organized well   Yes   No
    Consistent theme follows throughout entire website   Yes   No
    Readability makes good use of chunking text and limited scrolling   Yes   No
    Colors used in an attractive and nondistracting manner   Yes   No
    Fonts are standard or at least easy to read in contrast to page colors   Yes   No
Based on the information above this site:
    Should be kept for future use_____
    Should be bookmarked for possible use_____
    Should not be used again_____
Comments:

Figure 5.1.   Website Evaluation Rubric

Finally, the design of the site needs to be considered. Although good design doesn't mean that the content will be accurate, it should be a factor in terms of usability and in actually finding the information the student needs. If two sites are considered equal in terms of content, then naturally the better-designed site might be the best choice. There are additional aspects to consider when evaluating sites for students with disabilities. For example, poor choice of colors could make it difficult for someone who's colorblind, a small font over a graphic might be hard for someone with poor eyesight to read, and sound that doesn't have accompanying text description can't be understood by someone who's deaf.

To evaluate websites accurately, students need to be taught what to look for and should begin from an early age building these skills. Therefore, the teacher or librarian can adjust the same rubric and the types of lessons based on the age and skill level. A younger student might only use a checklist with a couple points, while an older high school student could use a very detailed and expansive guide. Furthermore, a teacher who is using a website for an entire class might examine a website more thoroughly than a student who's only concerned about it for their own uses and for a one-time project. A website that's put on the library Web page should very clearly be identified as an appropriate site. At times only a portion of a site is worthwhile, but that's OK. What matters is that there's something worthwhile for the end user. On the other hand, you want to be sure that the links on the websites don't go to any objectionable places. It's possible that a website with, for example, 100 links might have one or two mixed in that aren't a good choice for your students to visit. What exactly those sites contain might determine if the first site is still able to be used.

One way to teach students about evaluating websites naturally includes discussing these evaluation forms. The different aspects to the website can be explained with helpful information for students to follow. This is usually followed by talking about search engines and then finding a site to evaluate.

Another alternative is to intentionally show students Web pages that are misleading. These bogus sites might at first glance look valid, and only upon a closer inspection can students detect that the sites do break some of the rules. Sometimes, the bogus sites look so real that it takes further research to figure out exactly why the content they provide is misleading.

WEBQUESTS

The Web has matured to a point where it's not a question of if it should be used in the library and the classroom but instead how best to incorporate it into learning strategies. While the use of the Web as a communication or information tool can be in an unstructured format for general research or as an additional resource, it can also be structured as part of a lesson planned around Web resources. One such type of lesson is in the form of a WebQuest.

WebQuests were originally developed by Bernie Dodge, a professor at San Diego State University, as a model for integrating the use of the Web in classroom activities. A WebQuest is an inquiry-oriented activity in which some or all of the information that learners interact with comes from Internet resources. The teacher (and/or the librarian) prepares or finds a

WebQuest ahead of time for students to use as part of a class lesson. This consists of a website that the student searches by following the information and the links on the pages as a self-contained lesson. Since the lesson is on the Web and contains the content and links to more content, it's highly portable and easy to access—versus buying and installing computer software. Although it takes time to develop a WebQuest, the technical skills required are only those of a basic Webmaster.

The heart of the WebQuest is scaffolding. From a cognitive psychology perspective, newly acquired information that the students acquire while on their WebQuest builds upon what they've learned already. Information is presented in an orderly manner that students can follow independently or in small groups and then transform, or integrate, the new information based on what they have learned in the past. In this sense, the novice is encouraged to take on the role of a more advanced learner.

Can a WebQuest be done without the Internet? Yes, but the technology makes it easier to create on the Web. Students have always been provided with packets of information, reading lists, annotated bibliographies, and access to resources in a physical library. This is a structured environment that replicates finding and using electronic resources in today's libraries. WebQuests are a great format for librarians to use to teach students information literacy skills.[10]

Although WebQuests can naturally vary quite a bit, there's a basic structure that ensures that students can follow the lesson. This includes six sections: Introduction, Task, Resources, Process, Evaluation, and Conclusion.[11]

Real WebQuests pass the ARCS filter: Does the activity get students' Attention? Is it Relevant to their needs, interests, or motives? Does the task inspire learners' Confidence in achieving success? Would completing the activity leave students with a sense of Satisfaction in their accomplishment?[12] Sending students on a WebQuest simply to fill time or to keep students busy is a disservice. Librarians want to ensure that if a WebQuest is used, it's a quality website and is used effectively in conjunction with related activities.

When a WebQuest poses an open-ended question, students must do more than "know" facts. Open-ended questions activate students' prior knowledge and create a personal curiosity that inspires investigation and brings about a more robust understanding of the material. To create this curiosity, the teacher and librarian can use several strategies. Some include asking students to apply lessons from global problems to local issues, asking students to use their assigned perspectives to predict near-future outcomes of current events, or asking students to argue why a particular option will thrive best in a given situation.[13]

WebQuests are also a good way for librarians and teachers to collaborate. Talking about the subject, finding resources, and especially discussing the teaching aspects of creating your own site brings people together to look at the different perspectives. Although you can find and use what others have created by searching the Web or you can create something very specific to your own needs, it is a great opportunity to help teachers select resources.

VIRTUAL FIELD TRIPS

Another type of Web-based activity in which students are guided along a predetermined path is virtual field trips. Virtual field trips allow students to see and experience a place that they would never be able to physically visit because of transportation costs, time, or even safety issues. These websites are multimedia experiences, consisting of camera images and accompanying text descriptions at a minimum. More developed sites might also include video and audio.

A field trip can be organized in many different ways depending on the purpose of the website or the preferences of the author. It may consist of a linear event with the student moving from one event to the next, or it might be much more flexible with the student deciding upon which hyperlinks to follow based on their own interests.

Many teachers and librarians find existing virtual field trips that others have created and simply incorporate them into their lessons like any other website. Sometimes they're created by themselves or people that they know, such as a family member. It's not uncommon for teachers to take a digital camera on a vacation or some other type of trip, keep a journal for notes, and then assemble a website to share their experiences with students. Or family and friends might visit another country, which would provide a very personal experience to share.

WEBSITES

LM_NET: www.eduref.org/lm_net
The WebQuest Page: http://webquest.org/index.php

Database Vendors

BrainPop: www.brainpop.com
CQ.com Products: www.cq.com
Dialog: www.dialog.com

EBSCO: www.ebscohost.com/
Facts on File: http://factsonfile.infobasepublishing.com/newsservices.asp
Google Docs: docs.google.com
LexisNexis: www.lexisnexis.com
NetLibrary: www.netlibrary.com
OCLC: www.oclc.org
OVID: www.ovid.com
ProQuest: www.proquest.com
Stat-USA: www.stat-usa.gov
Thomson Gale: www.gale.cengage.com/
United Streaming: http://streaming.discoveryeducation.com/
Wilson: www.hwwilson.com

Evaluation

ALA Great Websites for Kids Selection Criteria: www.ala.org/ala/alsc/great
    websites/greatwebsitesforkids/greatwebsites.htm
CyberBee Web Evaluation: www.cyberbee.com/guides_sites.html
Evaluating a Site: www.netknowhow.ca/nkhSRevaluate.html
Kathy Schrock's ABC's of Website Evaluation: http://kathyschrock.net/
    abceval/index.htm
Online Writing Guide for Students: http://classweb.gmu.edu/nccwg/web
    critique.html
Web Pages That Suck: www.webpagesthatsuck.com

Bogus Websites

Aluminum Foil Deflector Beanie: http://zapatopi.net/afdb/Ban Dihydrogen
    Monoxide: www.lhup.edu/~dsimanek/dhmo.htm
Dihydrogen Monoxide Research Division: www.dhmo.org
Feline Reactions to Bearded Men: www.improb.com/airchives/classical/cat/
    cat.html
GenoChoice: www.genochoice.com
The Jackalope Conspiracy: www.sudftw.com/jackcon.htm
MoonBeam Enterprise and Lunar Travel Agency: www.dreamweaverstudios
    .com/moonbeam/moon.htm

Course Management Systems

Blackboard: www.blackboard.com
eCollege: http://ecollege.com
Moodle: http://moodle.org/

NOTES

1. "It All Started with Babbage," *Computerworld* 39, no. 31 (August 1, 2005): 28.

2. Paul Baran, "On Distributed Communications Networks," *IEEE Transactions on Communications Systems* CS-12, no. 1 (March 1964): 1–9.

3. *Collins Dictionary of Computing* (2000), "Internet," www.xreferplus.com/entry/ 1253681 (accessed October 19, 2004).

4. Christos J. P. Moschovitis, Hilary Poole, Tami Schuyler, and Theresa M. Senft, *History of the Internet* (Santa Barbara, CA: ABC-CLIO, 1999), 161.

5. *Collins Dictionary of Computing* (2000), "WWW (World Wide Web)," www .xreferplus.com/entry/1256208 (accessed October 19, 2004).

6. Allen C. Benson, *Neal-Schuman Complete Internet Companion for Librarians* (New York: Neal-Schuman, 2001), 7.

7. *Collins Dictionary of Computing* (2000), "Email or e-mail," www.xreferplus .com/entry/1252851 (accessed October 19, 2004).

8. Linda Roberts, "Harnessing Information Technology for International Education," *Phi Delta Kappan* 86, no. 3 (November 2004): 226.

9. Roberts, "Harnessing Information Technology," 226.

10. Linda Braun, "In Virtual Pursuit," *School Library Journal Net Connect* (Fall 2001): 32–34.

11. Braun, "In Virtual Pursuit," 32–34.

12. Tom March, "The Learning Power of WebQuests," *Educational Leadership* 61, no. 4 (December 2003): 44.

13. March, "The Learning Power of WebQuests," 45.

6

School Library Websites

Although some school libraries don't have websites, it's becoming rarer. Recent surveys indicate that close to 90 percent of school librarians maintain websites.[1] This number will surely rise to near 100 percent over the next few years because of the variety of options we now have. So rather than asking whether the library should have a site or not (as was the case a decade ago), the questions today are about how to organize the existing sites, what features to include, and how to keep it updated, considering all of the other important tasks the average librarian must handle daily. Maintaining a school library website to present information and organize links has become an expectation of the job just as common as maintaining a book collection with an online catalog. The library website is the point of access to electronic resources the library subscribes to or owns; the way to find print resources; and a place to share news, information, policies, and other documents.

The advantage of the library website is the immediacy of updates. Information and materials, print or electronic, are much more fluid than in the past. The ability to update the website and provide a place to locate resources as soon as they change is more important than ever. Furthermore, the ease with which students and teachers can access this information from multiple locations means not having to produce physical items like pathfinders that sit in a rack in the library.

The literature in this respect has been limited when focused on school libraries. If you look at website creation in a broad sense, you can find quite a lot of information that would be applicable to your needs: technical issues, design, organization, color, usability, and on and on. When it comes to specifics of school libraries, much of the literature tends to turn back to those general issues. There is, however, some good information that deals specifically with website-creation issues that school librarians would be concerned about, with some in-depth sources about what features to include. For instance, Diane Caro explains that a school library website should provide current information to students from numerous sources through hyperlinks to other websites and databases with full-text articles.[2] Furthermore, school library websites can also enable communication between students, librarians, and teachers.

School libraries have different aims and purposes for developing their websites. These varied purposes reflect the numerous individuals using the site (students, teachers, parents, library staff, parents of prospective students, and people outside the school).[3]

Walter Minkel provides some specific ideas about what to include on a school library website.[4] Minkel recommends including links to specific teacher assignments, bibliographic aids, the library catalog, databases, and local institutions (museums, zoos, parks, historic sites), as well as your name and how people can contact you. However, Minkel cautions that simply providing a list of links is not enough. In doing so, librarians aren't following their own advice, demonstrating that "librarians often don't act like librarians."[5] Many websites are disorganized, lack sufficient information, and are not much more than a list of links.

WEB EDITORS AND HTML

When choosing what software to use to create and maintain a school library website, the program choices are the same as those used more commonly by Web designers in general. There might be a schoolwide or district policy as to what can be used, in which case no decision needs to be made. While this is often the case so that licensing costs can be reduced or so that standardization is applied throughout computers on the network, it's usually more of a matter of preference for those involved in overseeing technology. In reality, several different choices would work fine. The tool itself is not what's important. What's important is how you use the tool. This is why instruction, for yourself and/or for your students, in Web design should focus on concepts and principles, as opposed to simply where to point the mouse.

Although text editors are almost never used today, not long ago this was the only option. Today, the major products in terms of Web editors include Adobe Dreamweaver and free or open-source options, such as Nvu or Mozilla SeaMonkey. Dreamweaver is the most expensive and has the most features; it's considered the standard among Web developers. For some librarians, when cost is a major factor and budgets are tight, the free alternatives will get the job done. Additionally, some school websites are built upon a proprietary XML-based structure in which a provided form based editor is the only option for creating and updating pages. In this case, special training and editing privileges must be provided.

An interesting alternative that requires no programming skills is the use of Blackboard or other course-management software, such as Moodle or eCollege. If the school already uses such software for distance learning or classroom collaboration, it's an easy place to create a course for library resources. Although the structure of the course might not be as flexible as an individually created website, it does make an easy way to share links, documents, lessons, resources, and a great deal of information. Furthermore, because students already have to log on to the system via password, it's a place where you can post additional passwords for library databases for home use if you don't have a proxy server. This way, students need only remember a single login instead of several. A simple library website in combination with a full Blackboard course can provide complexity and resources with little cost and less training.

Additionally, wikis can also be utilized to create the entire library website or portions of it. This gives the librarian complete control as well as access from any location. Again, there will be some limitation in layout and design, but the benefits may outnumber the disadvantages.

WEBSITE HOSTING

According to Anne Clyde,[6] there are several options for the creation and maintenance of the school library website. The site can be

- created in-house by the school library staff (the most common scenario);
- created and managed by someone from outside the school;
- created by someone from outside but maintained by school library staff;
- created as part of an integrated school website;
- created centrally at the district level; or
- created partially or entirely by students.

Today, approximately 76 percent of all librarians maintain their own sites. The 24 percent that don't have someone else fill that role. In order from most to least common, this person could be some type of technology technician, a teacher, a student(s), a library aide, the school webmaster, district office personnel, the principal or an administrator, or parent volunteers. Although there's nothing wrong with having others help with website maintenance and creation, sites over which the librarian doesn't have direct control tend to be more limited in scope and don't hold up to the rigors required.

DESIGN/USABILITY

Designing the look and feel of the school library website can sometimes be the hardest part. Ideally, you want to sketch out the design of the site before you even start. It's much easier to do this ahead of time rather than having to go back later to redesign after realizing that a change needs to be made throughout. Whether you use a program like Inspiration, a word processor, or simply pieces of paper, you need to visualize the content for the site and how it will be organized, with a specific set of initial pages.

One of the issues to keep in mind is your audience. A library Web page for a third grader will be much different than that for a high school student. This poses additional demands for schools that cover a large range of grades, such as a K–12 or even a K–8. Depending on the range of grades, there may have to be different branch-off points. A common home page with links to home pages for different age groups is one way around this dilemma.

If a school or district has a template that you are required to follow, you'll have to learn how to work within these confines. This can be especially difficult if the template uses a large menu that takes up valuable top and/or side screen space, in which case you need to have another level of menu headings for your own library pages. Teachers who make their own class websites may also run into these issues, so it is something to discuss with the school as a whole in terms of which elements are required and which aren't.

Besides a navigation bar, in some other areas, the school might want you to conform, including font choice, colors, graphics, and more. Colors can pose an additional problem as you want to ensure that the pages are readable, as opposed to simply good looking. Just because a school has certain school colors doesn't mean that they have to overwhelm the Web page design. Elegant emphasis with those colors on a page with white background and black text can add a touch of school identity yet still leave the overall design open and usable.

Furthermore, younger children can be overwhelmed by large, complex pages with a lot of choices and reading, and text with small font sizes that may appear attractive to adults may be difficult for young children to navigate with the mouse pointer. Remember that what works for adults might not be best for kids. On a related issue, database descriptions and names may not always be as clear, especially for younger students. Provide alternative names and organize them so that students are easily aware of what they should be using. Simply having a link to "ERIC" (Educational Resource Information Center) would make no sense to many students—even though we know that it's the premier database for citations to educational journals and documents. Keep the end user in mind.

Finally, Americans with Disabilities Act issues must also be kept in mind. While it might be difficult to design around disabilities, small things can be done with little or no effort. For instance, be sure to provide alternate text for images so that students with vision problems can read what the image is, don't use colors that will be difficult for someone who's colorblind to see, and if you use any sound clips be sure to include a textual transcript for students with hearing problems.

FEATURES

A common way to make decisions about your own website is by looking at other sites. You can gain technical knowledge and ideas not only about design and organization but also about specific categories and features to include. Because a single person can only realistically browse through a small number of other sites, a Web designer can only discover and incorporate a fraction of the possibilities that are out there. Therefore, studies that collect data from large numbers of people are needed to provide the greatest amount of information. The following information can be used as a guide to see how your site fits in with everyone else, show areas where it is lacking, give you ideas, or even reaffirm that you and your administrators are already on the right track. Regardless of the state of your website, there are a lot of ways to use this data.

One particular study consisted of a Web-based 54-question survey.[7] The first part of the survey consisted of nine background questions. It provided information about the schools, librarians, and the situation at that specific school library.

The first question simply asked if the library had a website. It was used as a way for participants who didn't have a library website to exit the survey. The results show that 87 percent of LM_NET respondents to the survey did have an existing library website.

Another question asked about the experience level of the librarian to find if experience had any impact on decisions. Results were spread out among the categories, with 26 percent having 4 or less years of experience, 20 percent with 5 to 9 years, 32 percent with 10 to 20 years, and 22 percent with 21 years or greater. All types of libraries were represented, with 25 percent being elementary, 19 percent middle school, 42 percent high school, and the final 15 percent a combination of the others. In terms of location, 28 percent of the schools were in rural areas, 48 percent suburban, and 24

Table 6.1.   Basic Features

Feature	Percentage Found
E-mail address of librarian	90
Employees listed	79
Webmaster contact information	79
Phone number of library	76
Mailing address of library	73
Hours open/closed	72
Date website last updated	69

percent urban. Thirty-four states and Canada were represented. Staffing was also what one would expect, with 88 percent reporting that they had one FTE (full-time equivalent) librarian or less for their school and 82 percent that they had one FTE paid support staff or less.

The next section of the survey asked about basic features found on these types of websites regardless of their specific purpose (see table 6.1). This was meant to give an indication about the commonality of school librarians in following good Web protocol. From an information literacy viewpoint, these features are often what we tell our students to look for when determining if a website should be considered when doing their own research. Overall, most school library websites did a good job reflected by the high percentages. The highest was an e-mail address at 90 percent and the lowest was 69 percent for date last updated.

The next section of the survey asked about features that would tend to be more specific to school library websites (see table 6.2). Some were found at the majority of sites (class resources, databases, policies, mission statement, and library news), while other features that would seem to be popular just didn't get listed as often (calendar, OPAC [online public access catalog],

Table 6.2.   Library-Specific Website Features

Feature	Percentage Found
Class resources	74
Databases	70
Policies	57
Mission	53
Library news	51
Calendar/schedule	44
Award sites	39
OPAC	39
New acquisitions	24
Equipment available	21
Print journal list	17

award sites, new acquisitions, equipment available for use, and a print journal list).

Because a large portion of websites are meant to be a way to collect, organize, and share links to other sites, a series of questions asked about different categories (see table 6.3). The first question asked if the site contained a list of links, and a majority of 82 percent said that it did. The most popular category of links was a list of search engines that the students could choose from (78 percent). Other categories on a majority of sites included reference, a general list by subject, research guides, homework help, news/newspapers, teacher sites, and government. Those found at less than half included online magazines, fun sites, librarian links, health, career/college, and weather.

Finally, a section of the survey asked about other features found on the website. Results in any given category were limited, but they provided insight into some of this variance among webmasters. Prior to the formal analysis of school library websites, one might have assumed that all of the features listed in table 6.4 would be popular. In reality, the survey results showed a great variance in the prevalence of these features. The results ranged from the highest responses for bibliography help and instructional materials to others, such as special library events, author pages, copyright information, WebQuests, accelerated reader, pathfinders, book clubs or fairs, and parent volunteer information (see table 6.4).

The survey concluded with two open-ended questions so that respondents could talk about anything that the rigid survey couldn't cover or might have missed. The first asked about other features that their website

Table 6.3. Links School Library Websites Often Contain

Feature	Percentage Found
Simple list of links	82
Search engines	78
Reference	70
Websites by subject	67
Research guides	66
Homework help	58
News/newspapers	57
Teacher sites	56
Government	50
Online magazines	49
Fun sites	47
Librarian-specific links	46
Health	44
Career/college	37
Weather	25

Table 6.4.   Additional Content Often Found

Feature	Percentage Found
Bibliography help	63
Instructional materials	54
Special library events	43
Author pages	34
Copyright information	32
WebQuests	30
Accelerated Reader	28
Pathfinders	26
Book club/fairs	23
Parent volunteer info	15

includes that they would like to note. This list provides ideas that might have been hard to classify in other categories, items that might need to stand on their own, or simply neat ideas that others might want to consider in the future. These include the following:

- Ethnic groups pages
- Book reviews
- Lunch menu and sports scores ("helps draw kids to the site and kids then make our site their startup page")
- Public libraries in the area
- Computer lab schedule
- Earthquake alerts (from a respondent in California)
- Intellectual freedom
- Virtual library tour
- State standards
- Web forms for comments
- Tutoring opportunities
- Reading lists
- Pictures
- Parent section
- Collaborative lesson plans

The second open-ended question asked about features librarians knew they wanted but hadn't had the opportunity to implement. This question generated a lot of feedback about issues with time and money. It wasn't necessarily a problem with lack of awareness or ability but larger issues that seemed to take things out of one's hands. Two of the most common features that librarians wanted but didn't already have are Web-accessible OPACs and a larger collection of current, quality links. Other items mentioned include interactive surveys, website counters, and Web-based request forms. Some of the respondents simply replied with the following:

- "We just have a hard time maintaining our website, since I'm the only library employee."
- "I would like to have more info and links, but simply do not have enough time to keep it up-to-date."
- "I would like to include my book catalog but the tech powers say it can't be done."

With any type of analysis done at this level, there are always questions about correlations between responses and groups of respondents. You might wonder if the number of years of experience, location, type of school, or amount of staffing made an impact. Although there were some connections, overall there were not that many. Most of the respondents had the same experiences and ideas. There were, however, some significant statistical Pearson correlations that came up with the question of who maintains the site. When the school librarian was listed as the primary webmaster, the site was more likely to include instructional materials (Pearson correlation coefficient of .244), class resources (.182), the name of the webmaster (.173), websites by subject (.173), WebQuests (.182), author pages (.182), and links to websites about government (.243) and news (.168). These are important findings, too, and need to be shared with school administrators. Librarians have important roles, and their expertise can't be replaced by others who don't have the same background. School librarians are important for the virtual aspect of the library as well as the physical.

In terms of significant Pearson correlations that would help to support the validity of the survey, there was a noted relationship between the number of librarians and the number of support staff (.190). Incidentally, it also showed that the type of library had an impact on staffing and that high schools tended to have more librarians and support staff (.217). The greater the number of librarians a school had, the greater the chance that the website would list new acquisitions (.218) and provide a print journal list (.230). It would seem that if more help is available, the school librarian has more time to add additional features.

The type of library also had some different results for certain features. These results must be taken into consideration because age levels will affect whether or not some features are viewed as important. Some of the features that reflected varying numbers based on type of library included library news, databases, career/college, fun sites, news, online magazines, research information, Accelerated Reader, author pages, bibliography help, book clubs, parent volunteers, and special library events.

Finally, it's not too surprising that Dreamweaver has such wide usage since it currently dominates the overall Web-design market. However, it's interesting to note that the free tools are being used by 5 percent of school librarians. For those schools that simply don't have the money, and for those school librarians that don't need a product that's too complicated, free has found a niche.

The results of this study show that a lot of progress has been made in school library websites. It's quite amazing how quickly school librarians, regardless of age, have learned new skills and adopted use of the Web and expanded their services. They're all quite aware of what they want to do next, and research like this can help to guide the development of future redesign and additions to current sites. It's apparent that there are issues of time, money, and internal control. For now, school librarians can see what others are doing and make a better case to their administrators about the resources they need.

Finally, the survey shows the supportive nature of school librarians today. The number of responses was higher than expected, and quite a few stated that they really appreciated the survey and plan to use it as a checklist as they update their own websites. The features listed clearly show that some are more common than others. Although each library is different, a librarian should start with some of the more basic features before moving onto some of the less-common ideas. Regardless, it's hoped that improvements to school library websites will benefit those who use them most: the children.

THE PROCESS

What exactly does all of this boil down to? First, you have to do your homework, whether you are creating a new site from scratch, redesigning an older site, or continuing work with an existing site. Find out your school district's requirements and processes. Choose a Web editor, get file space on the server, and set up the technical procedures. Meanwhile, decide exactly what you want to include on your site and begin gathering that information. Design the organization of the site, the number of pages, and how they'll connect. Don't be afraid to ask for feedback. Ask your colleagues, students, and friends to test run the site after you have it working to see if they have any difficulty understanding where things are.

Finally, this checklist will give you some ideas as to where you can start and what you may want to strive for later. It can be overwhelming to do everything at once, so if you design the entire organization of the site, you can always go back later to add more.

First Priority: Basic Website Features

- Mailing address
- Library or librarian e-mail address
- Library phone number
- Employees listed
- Hours open/closed
- Webmaster contact information
- Date website last updated

Second Priority: Library-Specific Website Features

- Mission
- Library news
- Policies
- Calendar/schedule
- New acquisitions
- Equipment available (e.g., digital cameras)
- Journal list (print journals subscribed to)
- OPAC
- Databases (paid subscription, full-text)
- Award sites (e.g., Caldecott)
- Class resources (for specific teachers or classes)

Third Priority: Links for School Library Websites

- Simple list of website links
- Websites by subject
- Search engines
- Career/college
- Fun sites
- Government
- Health
- Homework help
- News/newspapers
- Online magazines
- Reference
- Research guides or information
- Weather

- Teacher sites by discipline, topic, and/or grade
- Librarian-specific links

Fourth Priority: Additional Content for Expanded School Library Websites

- Accelerated Reader (or similar alternative)
- Author pages
- Bibliography help
- Book club/book fairs
- Copyright information
- Instructional or informational materials
- Parent volunteer information
- Pathfinders
- Special library events
- WebQuests

WEBSITES

Cynthia Says: www.cynthiasays.com/
International Association of School Librarianship, Creating a Web Page for Your School Library: www.iasl-online.org/advocacy/resources/creating web.html
Mozilla: www.mozilla.com
Nvu: www.nvu.com
School Libraries on the Web: www.sldirectory.com/index.html
SeaMonkey: www.seamonkey-project.org/
World Wide Web Consortium: www.w3.org

NOTES

1. Odin Jurkowski, "Schools of Thought: What to Include on Your School Library Website," *Children & Libraries: The Journal of the Association for Library Service to Children* 3, no. 1 (2005): 25.

2. Diane Caro, "School Library Website: This Virtual Library Is Always Open," *Colorado Libraries* 27, no. 3 (2001): 7–8.

3. Anne Clyde, "School Library Websites," *Teacher Librarian* 28, no. 2 (2000): 51–53.

4. Walter Minkel, "We're Not Just a Building," *Library Journal Net Connect* (Spring 2003): 26–27.

5. Walter Minkel, "It's Not Rocket Science: Making Your Site's List of Links Supremely Useful Isn't All That Difficult," *School Library Journal* 48, no. 6 (2002): 31.

6. Anne Clyde, "Creating the School Library Website," *Teacher Librarian* 29, no. 3 (2002): 25–28.

7. Jurkowski, "Schools of Thought," 24.

3

FROM THE LIBRARY TO
THE CLASSROOM

7

Equipment

Part 3 of this book looks at the technology in a school library and how it can be directly used and shared with teachers in the classroom. Chapter 7 covers some of the types of equipment that teachers may check out, and chapter 8 covers how librarians may help teachers directly in the classroom setting. The concept of librarian involved throughout the school is a growing role in which all benefit.

School libraries have always included a mixture of different devices, tools, and information formats. At passing glance, computers, books, and other printed materials make up the majority of library items. However, myriad other technologies are available, some more and some less expensive. The school library is the center point for technology in the school, with some stored in the library for use by teachers and students and some lent out to the classrooms. This handling of technology necessitates that the librarian understand the basics of using these tools and teaching others how to use them. The roles of instructional partner, instructional consultant, teacher, and trainer all play a part in the everyday work of the school librarian.

Historically, the school library has always been the dispenser of technology. What was once an audio/visual department with educational-technology ties has blended into the modern-day library. Whereas in the past a student might have rolled out a filmstrip projector to a classroom, today you're more likely to see a class checking out a digital camera or camcorder for use in a specific lesson. The school library could well be the place of both bookworms and tech geeks.

One of the most complicated aspects of talking about the technology in the school library is that it's difficult to separate technology that can be used in the classroom and in society at large. Just about everything you'll find is used elsewhere—even though each piece is used for educational purposes in slightly different ways. Therefore, discussion about school library technology blends in with school technology and educational technology.

To further complicate the issues, the technologies are constantly changing. We know all too well that it's difficult to keep up with the latest trends. Although this has been a continuing concern since the very first school library, it feels as if this pace has quickened. Our appetite for the latest and greatest tools, our desire to provide the best for our students, and corporations that want us to buy more of their products have created a never-ending cycle of purchasing and replacing our tools. This chapter might not include each and every piece of equipment found in school libraries across the country; it does speak about many of the basic technologies. Think about purchasing these things if you do not already have them.

This chapter provides some historical background on earlier technologies and an overview of the equipment found in most school libraries today. The focus isn't on computers (spoken about elsewhere in this book) but instead on the rest of the equipment housed in the school library.

HISTORICAL EQUIPMENT

To see where we are today, we need to understand where we have come from. Schools interested in using technology have to supplement, and even sometimes replace, teaching in the classroom. Indeed, the phonograph was initially seen as a teacher-replacement device and a cost-savings measure. Administrators pictured students sitting in a classroom listening to recordings made by the brightest educators. If students could learn from the use of this technology, then why pay for local teachers, they argued. Concepts of division of labor and mass production seemed to encourage this type of outsourcing. Of course, we now know that this never happened. Yet even today some people make similar arguments while trying to save money, talking about replacing libraries, librarians, and teachers with the Internet, computer software, and distance education.

Film

The first use of media in the classroom occurred in 1911 when Thomas Edison produced the earliest educational films. More of a novelty at first, films were slow in becoming widely used. The film projectors were complicated machines that weren't user friendly. Before 16-mm film was perfected, there were considerable fire hazards. Many laws prohibited the use of films in classrooms unless the rooms were equipped with fireproof booths. Therefore, with the combination of cost, safety, and the fear of teachers trying to use the earliest film projectors, this fledgling media took some time to become standard.

Those initial films were silent, merely providing video during which the teacher could talk the students through what they were watching. By the 1920s, the first educational films with sound were developed, although with mixed reactions.[1] Many feared that their silent equipment would become obsolete and useless, others wanted to wait and see if the new machines with sound would actually last or if they would be a short-lived novelty, and still others were resistant to changing their teaching style to accommodate the evolving technology. Sound familiar?

The biggest push for the evolving technology came from the military, as has often been the case with educational technology. By World War II, the military saw educational films as a way of speeding up training and standardizing instruction with less manpower and less cost. Schools benefited by the push for better and cheaper equipment and higher production levels used in creating these films.

Radio

As an alternative to film, radio was a popular yet short-lived experiment. Radios were less expensive and more reliable, and the same benefits of bringing in scholars and programming from elsewhere were seen as a way of reducing local costs and improving student learning. The main growth took place between 1925 and 1935 but then began to wane soon after and has all but disappeared.

The first development in educational radio was the Ohio School of the Air. Schools from around the country could tune in and listed to programming throughout the week, following the programming guides to determine the classes that would listen. Some of this programming included story plays; current events; history dramalogues; art appreciation; stories for younger pupils, intermediate grades, and upper grades; geography; high school dramatization of literature; music; and much more.[2] Soon after, NBC (the National Broadcasting Company), the American School of the Air, CBS (the Columbia Broadcasting System), and others provided additional programming. However, new technologies would evolve to take their place.

Television

The concept of delivering instruction via radio waves as well as through video and audio on films viewed in-house culminated in excitement for educational television. Today you're likely to see televisions in many, if not all, classrooms or at least available for use somewhere in the school.

In 1953, the first educational television stations were dedicated, and well-known stations such as WQED (channel 13) in Pittsburgh, KQED (channel 9) in San Francisco, and WTTW (channel 11) in Chicago were born. By 1956, formal instruction via television began at the college level; the Chicago city junior colleges, for example, experimented with offering nine complete courses taught each year on WTTW.

Programming was scarce at first, but Mr. Rogers began in 1967 on WQED and was later carried by PBS starting in 1968. With the development of *Sesame Street* in 1971, a new era began. *The Electric Company* followed in 1973 and *3-2-1 Contact* in 1980. Initially these programs were meant as a way to level the educational playing field and bring expert instruction to all. However, teachers found it difficult to incorporate the programming into their lessons, and it was difficult to schedule student days around the fixed time that they would have to tune in.

Historical Ramifications

Educational programming is still on radio and television. Although not education instruction in a strict sense, the programming could still be used in an educational setting; the move to more flexible physical media has made use of videotapes and DVDs more common. Contrast the use of these older technologies with today's satellite programming, cable television, streaming video, etc. The past 100 years has seen technologies continually evolving, which makes one wonder if we're really hitting a plateau or if we'll spend the rest of our careers having to readapt. What will our libraries and classrooms look like in another generation, and will they look back on our current technologies as novel experiments that never panned out? According to Saettler,

> Past history has clearly shown that before one technology can be developed in an orderly process for maximum efficiency, a new one appears on the horizon. Beginning with the instructional slide, a kind of media bandwagon syndrome has influenced educators' decisions about new media superimposed on the educational system implying that existing educational ills or problems could be cured by the use of this new medium or mode of technology.[3]

Although it's perfectly acceptable to get excited about new technologies and we need to continue to stay abreast of developments in order to bring the best educational experience we can to our students, we also need to temper this with some healthy questioning by keeping these historical trends in perspective. We need to be realistic regarding what the technology can do for us, and educate our administrators, teachers, students, and parents to limit misperceptions that could hurt our schools and libraries. We've not seen our teachers and librarians replaced by technology, and we need to ensure that it doesn't happen in the future.

MATURE TECHNOLOGIES

When we talk about technologies in the school library, we have to keep in mind that the term is very broad. Any type of device, tool, or piece of equipment used to enhance our abilities is technology. It's easy to forget that many of the things we take for granted today were technological marvels in the past. And many of these technologies would be difficult to live without today. In discussing mature technologies, I try to point out many of the tools that we take for granted. You'll see these tools in just about every school and used in conjunction with some of the more complex equipment included later in this chapter.

Take, for example, the common book. This incredible piece of technology is portable, stores a great deal of content, offers visual displays as well as text, has higher resolution than most monitors, is relatively inexpensive, is durable, and is user friendly.

The online catalogs that we now use are merely innovations based on common principles that have been around for quite some time. They were preceded by card catalogs, which were in turn preceded by book catalogs. Book catalogs, though they weren't updated frequently and couldn't display shelf status, were useful on college campuses as a way for students to see what books the library owned without having to actually walk to the library. Each stage in development has improved what we can offer to our students.

Furthermore, everything from the common pen, pencil, and paper can be seen as forms of technology in that through their use, information can be saved, retrieved, and shared with others. Chalkboards and whiteboards provide ways for educators to display information to an entire class at one time.

Older technologies include the traditional film strip projector, slide projector, and laserdisc player. These still might be used by an occasional teacher, but more than likely they have now been discarded or are simply being stored in a back cabinet. I continue to hear stories about librarians discovering some of this equipment when they start new jobs. Occasionally, a teacher finds some specific content irreplaceable and will not give it up. Others do not want to take the time to convert something as simple as a film slide to a PowerPoint presentation.

Teachers love to use some equipment in the library to prepare materials for class. This includes things like the popular laminator, lettering machine, spiral binding machine, and maybe even a large poster printer. Occasionally, you might find a portable wireless microphone for large gatherings. The library is the central location for equipment that can't be supplied individually for every classroom.

The library also needs to have a photocopier. A smaller school might not have any photocopiers in the rest of the building, but the copier in the library is always available. Whether the copier was bought by the library or rented on an annual contract, these costs and additional costs for paper and toner need to be spelled out so that they don't detract from the library materials budget.

The library and the entire school track the televisions, VCRs, and DVD players. Although records and phonographs will probably not be found, there could still be uses for tape players, cassette recorders, and CD players.

COMPUTER MEDIA

Storage devices in use with computers have evolved over time, and librarians and teachers have to deal with changing formats that have made older devices obsolete. Librarians will have to purchase their own storage media, often provide some to students on an as-needed basis, and possibly even supply this media to teachers and students as a repository for the school.

Some of the older media are certain to not be found in any modern library, and these include the 8-inch (100 kB), 5¼ inch (360 kB) floppies, and the 3½ inch (1.44 MB) floppy. Similar to the floppy, Zip disks (100-, 250-, and 750-MB versions) have also all but disappeared after a short time of wide use and flurry of potential. There have been other formats, but so many have come and gone so quickly that it's difficult to list them all.

Optical drives include recordable CDs (CD-R) and rewritable CDs (CD-RW), as well as recordable and rewritable DVDs (DVD-R and DVD-RW). Almost every computer today has a CD and/or DVD drive.

Libraries might also want to have USB flash drives available for purchase and/or borrowing because they have become the standard storage device as prices have continued to drop. Librarians need to be aware of these devices when arranging computers as students may be looking for the USB ports. Their price, storage capacity, and ubiquity means that these USB drives are likely to be used by students.

Some of this concern for providing and supplying storage media may dissipate over time as more schools push students to store files on the server instead of portable devices. Although this requires training and additional procedures, it does ensure that students won't lose these items. It also means that there's less concern with having to continually replace older devices with newer devices and with the different compatibility issues.

DIGITAL CAMERAS

Digital cameras are outselling traditional film cameras because of their versatility and ease of use. Prices have dropped considerably over the past few years, and quality and performance have made them alternatives for professional as well as everyday use. It's much easier for educators to snap a digital photo and move it into a computer program rather than get a roll of film developed and then scan the photographs one at a time. Libraries are the ideal place to store cameras and other equipment for teachers and students to check out and use. If your library has never purchased a digital camera before, then starting off with one or two would be a safe bet. Depending on how often they get used, you can determine if you'll need more to satisfy the demand. While checkout could be as simple as barcoding the camera case as with any book or other equipment, specific procedures and policies need to be put in place in case of damage or loss. While you don't want to hold students responsible for such high costs, there needs to be some type of assurance that the equipment is taken care of. This may necessitate some type of training or introduction to the use and handling of the equipment.

Digital cameras can be used for taking photos for inclusion on websites, PowerPoint presentations, handouts, student projects, and much more. This allows visual representation in lessons and can be introduced in just about any class.

With advances in digital camera technology, there's little distinction between the major manufacturers—Canon, Fujifilm, HP, Kodak, Nikon, Olympus, Sony, and Panasonic. Unless you buy a truly bottom-line, most have adequate resolution for today's needs. Although cameras can be bought with resolutions of ten or more megapixels, all you really need is about three. Anything above that is overkill for Web pages and PowerPoint presentations. In fact, the resolution of the monitor is so much lower that you can't even tell the difference. The main reason for greater megapixels is for very fine photo editing and enlarging small portions of an image. If you are just going to insert an image as is or if you are only going to do a simple crop, then a $100 to $200 camera will be fine.

Therefore, other considerations should be taken into account when deciding upon a model. This includes battery life (so that you can take plenty of pictures in a class without the battery dying), optical zoom as opposed to digital zoom (digital zoom creates a loss in resolution in order to manipulate the image and make it appear closer), LCD (liquid crystal display) size (so that you can easily see what you're taking a picture of), and size and weight. Because the camera would be used primarily in a classroom or a class setting, you might not want to spend more money for a smaller camera when a standard size will do just fine.

The biggest decision pertains to storage medium. Options include CD-R and CD-RW, CompactFlash, SD, xD, Memory Stick, and more. It depends on whether you want users to use a USB cable or docking station to transfer the photos to a computer or whether you want a physical medium to handle. Optical devices, such as CDs, are much more compatible, but most home users are accustomed to smaller cards like CompactFlash, SD, and Sony Memory Sticks. These hold quite a bit and are available in various sizes. You would be able to get by with a smaller memory size because the teacher would want to transfer the photos at the end of the day instead of storing weeks of work.

CAMCORDERS

Camcorders can also easily be stored and then checked out of the library. Media on VHS and 8mm tapes have all but disappeared. Today, like cameras, digital storage is the norm. Although a few models record directly onto DVDs, the same types of storage devices found in digital cameras are also used in video recorders. Some devices have permanent internal storage or a combination of internal and transferable storage. Some devices, like Flip Video Cameras, have made recording video, editing, and sharing easier than ever, and at a cost that makes them very attractive. Finally, a tripod would also be a good investment.

PROJECTORS

Different types of projectors have been a common fixture in classrooms for years. Everyone is familiar with the simple overhead projector, which consists of little more than a light source, a mirror, and a way of focusing the image from the transparency onto a screen or a wall. Although still in use today because of low cost, versatility, and teacher familiarity, projectors are in decline because of all of the opportunities we have with digital technologies.

Because multimedia projectors are much more expensive, not every classroom has one. The librarian can then be in the position of lending out projectors when needed, have one for lessons right in the library, be involved in the purchase of these machines, and train others to use them.

The two main technologies available are LCD and DLP (digital light processing). They produce roughly the same type of result in the classroom. Emerging technologies include the use of lasers, which will eventually reduce the size of these projectors even further since there'll be no need for a light bulb or for heat dissipation, but their development is still in the research phase. There's already talk about possible miniaturization that would one day allow a laser projector to be incorporated into a laptop computer with no visible increase in size or weight.

One of the common specifications is brightness, given in lumens. Multimedia projectors have matured, and almost all projectors will produce 1,000 lumens or more—all that most rooms will need. Two thousand lumens might be needed for a large auditorium or a very large classroom, but that amount is usually overkill. You need to consider that as the image size is increased, the light will become dimmer. You'll be competing against classroom lights and windows, but 1,000 lumens are usually enough.

A cost to consider is lamp life because light bulbs for projectors are very costly. While the projector itself costs anywhere from $1,000 to $3,000, replacement bulbs cost from $200 to $500 apiece. It's important to factor in these ongoing costs.

In terms of resolution, SVGA (super video graphics array; 800 × 600 pixels) and XGA (extended graphics array; 1024 × 768) are the most common. These will correlate fine with most computers. Higher resolution SXGA (super extended graphics array; 1280 x 1024) and UXGA (ultra extended graphics array; 1600 × 1200) are usually overkill.

Other factors should be considered. *Keystone correction* allows you to adjust for skewing of the image because of a height differential between the projector and the screen. *Throw distance* is the distance between the projector and the screen. Depending on the layout of the room, you might need to place the projector very close to the screen or very far away. You will want to adjust the size of the image on the screen regardless of where the projector sits. Some older projectors also have noisy fans, which can make it difficult to talk over. You'll want the fan, important for heat dissipation, to be whisper quiet. Finally, consider the size. Some projectors are extremely small, meant for travelers who have to carry them. This naturally boosts the cost. However, in a classroom setting, smaller is not always better. A larger and heavier machine on a cart is less likely to be knocked off or stolen. If security is a concern, you might also have to attach security cables between the projector and the mobile cart.

Another type of projector is a document reader. Whereas a traditional overhead projector displays transparencies and a multimedia projector displays images from an attached computer, a document reader displays whatever is placed under it. This would allow the entire class to see a close-up of

the object, anything from a rock or crystal in a science class to a page from
an historical text to a leaf.

PORTABLE COMPUTING DEVICES

Most classrooms have a computer or two, access to a computer lab, or
even access to a mobile laptop computer cart, but in certain instances
computing devices might be needed on a checkout basis. Some schools
have experimented with checking out laptop computers to students,
teachers, and classrooms, although buying the laptops can be costly and
maintenance and replacement costs are high. Nonetheless, having a few
laptops available can fill a need for many more users with specific circumstances.

Lower-cost netbooks are dominating computer purchases and will likely
become more prominent over the next few years. Being small, lightweight,
and inexpensive, more can be purchased for the same price of getting less
full-size laptops or desktops. The 10-inch screen size is most common, but
some are as small as seven inches. Once you get into the 12-inch range
you start approaching the size of laptops (typically between 14 and 17
inches).

An alternative is lower-cost PDAs (personal digital assistants). Their
prices are generally lower than computers, and their processing capabilities are growing by leaps and bounds. Beyond the simple functions of a
calendar or note-taking tool, PDAs can include word processors, presentation software, graphing capabilities, textbooks and reference materials,
math software and other educational software, and even phone and camera
functionality in the more robust models. Furthermore, their handwriting
recognition and simplification of features have made them much more user
friendly and capable compared to their earlier days. Numerous options can
be found for incorporating PDAs into classroom lessons.

Students who have been raised with technology are naturally attracted to
the portability of PDAs. Cellular phones, iPods, and video gaming systems
abound as students have adapted to small display screens and small but-
tons. The bulk of portable device use in education has been with PDAs,
although some universities have experimented with cellular phones, iPods,
and iPhones for delivering content and for interactivity.

Sometimes, however, a student wants to type a paper but doesn't need
an entire desktop computer or laptop. This is where such devices as AlphaSmart have found a niche. These word processors look like a cross
between a laptop and a PDA. They feature a full-sized keyboard, a small
display for reading and reviewing the text, easy connection to any com-

puter for transferring the text document, low cost, and greater durability than most other electronic devices. They are meant to inexpensively allow students to simply write wherever they want to. Whether in the classroom or at home, having this option could expand the opportunities for a greater number of students than with more expensive laptops.

Finally, with the rise of e-books, you might want to offer some type of e-book reader for students and teachers. Although this evolution is slower moving than the quick revolution predicted a few years ago, the movement hasn't stopped. With improving technology, better and greater content, and a realization that e-books are a supplement to and not a replacement of print, there's definitely the possibility of expanding your collection with these options.[4]

ASSISTIVE TECHNOLOGY

Assistive technology for students with disabilities is becoming more and more prevalent in school libraries and classrooms. This is due in part to the Americans with Disabilities Act, Section 504 of the Rehabilitation Act, and the Individuals with Disabilities Education Act. It's also because of a rising awareness of student needs and available solutions. Although it can be very expensive and difficult to accommodate all students, all librarians and teachers should at least try to accomplish the simplest solutions first. In the past, options were relatively few. These included large-print books, Braille, and audio recordings of texts. Low-tech solutions have also included pencil grips to make holding on to writing instruments easier. However, with increases in technology, more problems have been created. Solutions can still be found and the options have increased, and many of these alternatives simply require everyday awareness. For example, you can adjust the monitor resolution for students with poor vision; help students reach a book on a high shelf if they're in a wheel chair; or scan in a journal article, convert it with OCR (optical character recognition) software, and send the output to a speech synthesizer for blind students.

At a more complex level, several distinct categories of disabilities require certain solutions:[5]

- Communication disorders (nonspeaking children): allow children to communicate with others via text and images
- Visual impairments: handheld magnifier; larger print, brailled text; speech synthesizer; speech-recognition software, especially with today's use of Web pages and multimedia
- Hearing loss: hearing aids, real-time captioning

- Learning/cognitive impairments: predictive software for spelling, highlighted text and voice output, pencil grips
- Mobility impairments: alternative keyboard, speech recognition, trackball, and other alternative input devices
- Ergonomic issues: wrist pads, keyboards

WEBSITES

AlphaSmart: www.neo-direct.com/intro.aspx
Ebrary: www.ebrary.com
Flip Video: www.theflip.com
Intellitools: www.intellitools.com
Microsoft Accessibility: www.microsoft.com/enable
NetLibrary: www.netlibrary.com

NOTES

1. Paul Saettler, *Evolution of American Educational Technology* (Englewood, CO: Libraries Unlimited, 1990), 106.

2. Saettler, *Evolution of American Educational Technology*, 199.

3. Saettler, *Evolution of American Educational Technology*, 404–5.

4. Andrew Pace, "E-books: Round Two," *American Libraries* 35, no. 8 (2004): 74.

5. Cathy Bodine, "Assistive Technology and the Educational Process," *Colorado Libraries* 28, no. 4 (2002): 28.

8

Classroom Support

Many technologies have specific uses within the library, and many are found throughout the school and especially in the classroom. The school librarian and the library can provide direct support in the education and training in how to use technologies regardless of where they are housed or used. Often this is done directly in the library, and sometimes this means providing resources and equipment to teachers and bringing those tools into the classroom. Teachers may check out digital cameras or other equipment (as previously described). Further, teachers might need support with equipment that could find a familiar home in either a classroom or the library, such as multimedia projectors and other equipment. Sometimes, specific technologies are housed in classrooms or move between them.

This chapter focuses on equipment in the classroom that we, as librarians, may be asked to support and help in purchasing, and for which we may need to provide training in use. These devices may be found in a library, and while teachers have probably heard about them, they may not have direct experience or knowledge using them. School librarians can venture further into the realm of technology throughout the school and step into the classroom as a knowledgeable colleague. You'll want to be aware of the technology in the classrooms, both what teachers are and aren't using, so that you can better prepare to collaborate. Knowing the tools means that you can create lesson plans with information-rich resources to improve student learning. By reaching out to teachers in their classrooms, school librarians become effective learning specialists outside of the physical library realm.

The two primary technologies included in this chapter are mobile computer labs and electronic whiteboards. Although classrooms might still house some of the technologies already mentioned and require support from the school librarian for such items as TVs, VCRs, DVD players, and computers, this discussion of technologies is differentiated in terms of scope, size, and commitment. These primary technologies are thought of as truly school-wide technologies and don't have a library-specific connotation. They may as likely move among the classrooms or stay put. Teachers will still need support in finding and using information and library-related resources through access to the library website, online catalog, databases, other websites, WebQuests, and more. However, this is their turf. Teachers are not merely checking out a library camera, but instead feel ownership for the equipment. The relationship and the type of support therefore require the librarian to be comfortable in such a role.

The issue of support then leads to the question, how exactly do you assist? Because the classroom is truly outside of the library, who exactly is involved? Support will vary with the size of the school and the school's or district's determination of how many technology people they can provide. If the school doesn't have a specified technology support position, the librarian is usually the most technologically adept. Assuming that the library has a flexible schedule, additional staff to give assistance, and a school culture in which the administration and teachers look to the school librarian as a knowledgeable colleague who can provide support in purchasing and technology planning decisions, you may very well have a role to play.

Although less common, these predominantly classroom-based technologies could also be utilized in a library setting. The possibilities with an electronic whiteboard or a mobile laptop computer cart in the library are endless.

MOBILE COMPUTER LABS

There are two different mobile computing camps. In schools that have relatively high family incomes, students might be asked to purchase their own laptops. For instance, Town School for Boys, a K–8 independent school in San Francisco, requires families of fifth graders to purchase a laptop. In this case, the school is involved with determining models and software requirements so that there's some standardization for easier interoperability and especially so that the laptops interface well with the network and Internet access. This type of solution passes on the ownership and responsibility requirements to the students and teaches them to become stewards of their technology. These students are apt to take better care of the equipment and have a personal interest in utilizing the tools. They're quicker to use the various software programs in their daily regime.

A more common option is for the school to supply laptops on a mobile cart. As space for computer labs can be difficult to find unless part of new construction or a major renovation, these mobile carts allow every teacher and classroom to have the computer lab experience closer to where the teaching is actually taking place. Additionally, because the carts can move from room to room, a relatively small number of computers have to be purchased, and when they do need to be replaced, the process is simple. The advantages of this option include that it's easy to standardize the hardware and software and the only space required is a closet or the back of any room to keep the cart when not in use. The librarian could be part of the technology planning process, assist with troubleshooting, and advise how best to include library resources and incorporate the laptops into lessons.

With the prices of computers persistently falling, the continued positive public perception of computers in the schools, and the price and power differences between desktops and laptops diminishing, it's no surprise that one of every six U.S. school districts has some type of laptop program in place.[1] It appears that this trend will continue as the concept of computing as a separate space falls in favor of incorporating computing into everyday use and lessons. Today, learning to use computers is less a lesson in and of itself, and more a by-product of learning how to best utilize the tools at hand. This transformation of learning with computers instead of learning how to use computers has shifted the location of the bulk of learning.

A technology specialist, when purchasing equipment, must consider the laptops themselves, their carts, and the accompanying school foundation.

A common mistake when buying laptops is to focus on price.[2] Although prices have continued to drop and even the least expensive computers are adequate in common circumstances, laptop programs require hardier specifications. For instance, because of the handling and abuse that computers experience when carried by young children, you want to be sure that your laptops are solidly built, with durable construction and tough magnesium alloy cases. Furthermore, the laptops should be lightweight so that smaller children can easily lift them; have a screen that can be viewed from different angles because the students are apt to work in groups; and have a long battery life. Ideally, the computers should have the capacity to be used throughout the day. A typical scenario might include the battery charge lasting the morning, a charging time during lunch or other breaks, continued use throughout the afternoon, and then a full charging overnight. Finally, the wireless card should be built-in so that it doesn't get lost or damaged when removed.

Computer carts are specifically designed for laptop programs and should also be considered carefully because they protect a large investment. First, determine the number of laptop bays you need. Carts frequently have 16, 24, or 30 bays. Depending on budget and the size of the class, you might either want one computer per student or have them double up and share. Some carts might need more bays and others less if they are continually moving around the school.

The carts should also have large wheels with easy maneuverability so that they can be moved without losing control. A strong and secure cabinet with locks is vitally important for storage overnight and at times when the computers aren't in use. Finally, the cart also serves as a charging station, so laptops should be easy to plug in, with good power strips and power connections.

Outside of the actual cart and laptops, there are other aspects to consider. To begin with, a good wireless foundation needs to be built. However, if the building isn't wireless, then a local wireless network can be created from the cart itself. The cart can include a wireless access point to cover all of the laptops in the room. The cart would then be physically plugged into the school network. This is what brings the library and the Internet into the classroom for complete accessibility to resources.

Preplanning is required to prepare the laptops before their first use. Decisions need to be made about what programs should be installed and what specific configurations should be set. All of the laptops should be exactly the same so that all students know what to expect if they use one computer one day and a different one the next. It's also easier for the teacher to know what the students are looking at as they help them navigate the systems. Furthermore, it's much easier to prepare a single installation CD with all of the programs and everything set for ease of setup and reinstallations if something goes wrong.

Although the software will vary depending on the needs of the school, the classroom, and the individual teachers, the basics usually include an office suite with word processing, presentation, and spreadsheet capabilities. With these programs, a wide variety of lessons can be created. Then you will need a Web browser and accompanying plug-ins. Additional programs to round out basic needs include concept mapping and any other software from specific teacher requests.

Before implementation, it's important to provide enough professional development so that the teachers are comfortable and prepared for incorporating the laptops into classroom lessons. There should be some type of parent orientation so that they know what to expect and can prepare the students also. The technology staff should prepare a system for individual student usernames and passwords so that each student can easily log onto the network, and network space should be provided to store files. This reduces the need for removable media that can be lost or damaged.

The organization of the classrooms also needs to be considered as the use of computers will alter interaction between students and teachers. Desks and tables need to be arranged so that students can work together in small groups and move around as needed. On the other hand, students might sometimes need to work individually. Therefore, a flexible and moveable room should be prepared. This concept of small and unobtrusive classroom management is already being implemented in some of today's classrooms.

There'll always be questions from the community and from administrators about visible learning results when money is involved. One of the problems with convincing others that implementation of a laptop program is a good move is that little empirical evidence shows that it makes any difference. Current studies have failed to show a marked improvement on standardized achievement tests.[3] However, indications are that this is more likely because of the problem with standardized tests and what students are assessed on. There's evidence that computers, especially with a lower computer-to-student ratio, can motivate students and increase collaboration and learning. This is difficult to measure in simple multiple-choice tests.

When laptops are introduced, more project-based learning is incorporated, with higher rates of peer mentoring. Student motivation is increased. While this is also true of lower student-to-computer ratios, with laptops this appears to occur earlier, is more pronounced, and has been even more dramatic with special education and ESL (English as a second language) students.

In this type of learning environment, education is transformed. There's a pronounced increase in collaborative learning, students are more self-directed, and teachers can move around the room. Teachers are more apt to alter assessment techniques. With the guarantee that the technology is available on a more consistent basis, they're more willing to assign presentations and multimedia products to students with customized project-driven rubrics, and lessons lead to an emphasis on process, as opposed to simple assessment. Students are highly engaged. Mastery is no longer solely the province of technology gurus. Students tend to seek and offer advice to each other across grade levels and content areas. Productivity increases as students become better organized and use calendar programs. There's also been evidence that attitudes toward writing improve.

INTERACTIVE WHITEBOARDS

Chalkboards are still used in some of today's classrooms, but you won't find them in new construction, and they have been slowly replaced with whiteboards over the years. Chalk dust is not good for electronic devices and these problems only worsen over time. Whiteboards are often used in conjunction with multimedia projectors. Indeed, because whiteboards are flat and white, some teachers simply display the projector image directly on the whiteboard. This saves money, time, and space, and even allows the teacher to annotate the image by writing on the whiteboard. The next logical step was to make this setup even more interactive.

An interactive whiteboard is four presentation tools in one. There are several different vendors and models, but the basic concepts are the same. These tools can be used as a traditional whiteboard, projector screen, electronic copy board, or at the board's full potential, they can be connected to your projector and computer as an interactive whiteboard. By combining these components, this turns a computer and projector into an interactive teaching, collaborating, and presentation tool.

The major feature of the interactive whiteboard is its ability to be touch sensitive. Therefore, when a projector displays an image on the whiteboard, teachers and students can interact with whatever is shown either by use of the computer or by simply touching the "screen." These devices can be used in the library for instruction as well as in the classroom. Librarians, with their technical expertise, might be called upon to train teachers in using these tools, should be available for troubleshooting, and can help in determining what exactly to purchase.

Interactive whiteboards, by being touch sensitive, allow the user to use a finger as the mouse or keyboard. Some models use special pens or devices for this interaction, allowing colors, erasers, and special highlighting features. Floating tool palettes, menu boxes that can be moved around the screen (as opposed to locked in place), make for a high degree of markup and interaction. More complicated software has built-in optical character-recognition capability so that handwritten text can be converted to machine-readable text for ease in manipulation and saving. The concept is that teachers and students can walk up to the board and easily manipulate the display and also the software program without having to stand behind a computer. It brings a sense of deeper interaction with the environment.

The size and setup of interactive whiteboards vary considerably and depend on what the school can afford and the specifics of the classroom. These boards are available in sizes from 47 inches to 72 inches diagonal. This might seem small for someone who is used to a wall-sized screen. However, because the board is interactive, you need to be able to physically touch any portion of the screen. Therefore, you can't have a board that reaches the ceiling. Additionally, the larger the board, the more expensive it is.

Additional considerations include deciding upon a wall-mounted display or a display with a floor/table stand. The benefit of the wall-mounted display is that it's permanently fixed and ready to go when you need it. It's also more secure and less prone to damage or theft. The mobile display is placed on a stand and makes it easy to move from room to room. Therefore, a couple interactive whiteboards could meet the needs of an entire school, depending on how often they're needed. However, it would need to be determined when each class will have them and a storage place will need to be found. Furthermore, because there's no fixed distance between the board and the projector, it will need to be properly aligned each time so that you will be touching the correct area of the screen that the projector is showing and that the computer recognizes.

Finally, you need to be sure that the proper height is set so that all of your students can touch each part of the board. If the whole purpose is to make the experience interactive, and to ensure that students can come up to the front of the class to contribute and touch the screen, you might have to lower the board or you might need to install a stable, safe platform for students to step on to reach the board. Furthermore, the location of the board is also important to consider. While we usually think of a screen in the front of the class, it's possible to put it anyplace you want. Depending on the setup of your room, arrangement of desks, and location of fixed items throughout the room, there'll be many different ways of organizing this layout.

Another factor to consider is the direction of the projection. Interactive whiteboards, similar to other types of displays, have either front or rear projections. The front projection is more common, with a traditional multimedia projector in the back of the room, either mounted to the ceiling or sitting on a cart, showing toward the front of the room onto the board. The rear projection is usually reserved for a fixed, in-the-wall system, although it can also be used on a mobile stand. Rear projection is the same concept as a television screen or computer monitor, whereas front projection resembles movie theater projection. The rear projection is much more expensive, although as prices drop this type might become more common. The problem with the front projection is that the light from the projector shines right on the person and creates a shadow. This also means that the person writing on the board won't see what they are blocking. Furthermore, the light from the projector will shine in the eyes of the person at the board. For this reason, keep in mind the light output of the projector. Only use the minimum light output. A typical projector with 1,000 lumens (a measure of brightness) is adequate and average for classrooms. If this is not bright enough, it's recommended that you use blinds on the windows and lower the lights instead of using a brighter projector. You would also want to remind students not to look at the projector when they are working at the board. Because a rear projector doesn't have any of these problems, it's much easier to use if you can afford it.

When determining if an interactive whiteboard would be a good solution, you must consider if the rooms you will be using are ready as is and how they might need to be modified. Beyond room layout and organization already described, you must leave additional space around and in front of the board so that teachers and students can get to the board to write on it. This buffer space is more necessary than for a simple screen. So you need to plan for the computer, the projector, and an interactive whiteboard that's low enough for students to write on yet high enough that all the students can see what's happening. If you plan to use the multimedia capabilities to their maximum, you might also need speakers for sound. Security issues need to be addressed regarding when the room is unoccupied or when you're done using the interactive whiteboard. Finally, many of these organizational issues are difficult to work around if you have limited network jacks and electrical outlets. Although longer cables and power cords are a temporary fix, they increase the likelihood that people will get hurt or equipment damaged if someone trips over these wires. The best solution is to ensure that the building is properly wired. This is an additional expense, but it comes with the territory of using this type of equipment.

When the basics have been considered, then you can start thinking about the available options and whether they would be useful. For instance, a popular option is a wireless pad or mini whiteboard that the teacher can carry around the room. This frees the teacher from being locked behind a computer desk. The teacher can spend time in front of the interactive white board and then walk around the room while the students interact. This increases hands-on teaching and individual attention.

Several companies, each with their own strengths and weaknesses, offer interactive whiteboards. SMART is probably the best known, but other alternatives include Activboard, Diamond, Hitachi, Interwrite, and Mimio. Cost is often a determining factor, but you also have to consider what the teachers will do in their rooms. Don't pay for overkill if the teachers will never use all of the features.

Motivation

Teachers have been very interested in using interactive whiteboards and other high-tech devices since the early 1990s, and one of the main reasons for this is simply because of increased student motivation. While studies have found it difficult to prove whether this technology can actually boost grades, they do seem to indicate that it can improve students' attitudes toward learning.[4] The more visually stimulating the tools, the more multimedia is included, and the more that students can directly interact with the technology, the more often their attention is held. Connecting to the Internet and integrating software programs can already be done, but the degree of interaction increases when students feel that they can touch what they're seeing.

Teachers also like the ability to prerecord class notes and homework assignments. Students who miss school have an easier time getting information presented in class, and teachers who know ahead of time that they will be absent can present substitute teachers with a greater amount of materials to work with—all because electronic whiteboards allow notes and assignments to be prerecorded.

Another benefit of using an interactive whiteboard is that students become active participants in learning.[5] It can stimulate their thinking. By using highlighting and emphasizing the display, students are more apt to understand. In this sense, the whiteboard presents a truer assessment of understanding than static pencil-and-paper examples. Another important feature is real-time interactivity with the Internet because the interactive whiteboards are often used to display websites.

An often-forgotten aspect or something not thought of in respect to interactive whiteboards is their ability to meet the needs of certain students with disabilities.[6] Because the U.S. deaf population communicates using American Sign Language, visual contact is important. Teachers can't turn their back to the room or sit at a computer and not look at all of their students. Instead, they must be at the front of the room so that the entire class can see sign language. An additional piece of software from SMART called SychronEyes takes this one step further by allowing the teacher to control student computers. It's hard to get the attention of deaf students when they're hard at work staring at their computers, but with control over the student computer screens, the teacher can display a message to look to the front of the classroom. This feature can also be worthwhile for students without disabilities.

The uses for an interactive whiteboard are almost limitless. From overhead transparencies to a multimedia projector and computer to a truly interactive whiteboard, the degree of immersion in the lesson increases. Whether used a little or a lot, these tools have a place in any class. From language arts, where the teacher might use the whiteboard for some type of interactive storytelling or with concept-mapping software, to mathematics, where it can be used to visually demonstrate how to solve word problems, students can interact in more of a dynamic setting than ever before.[7]

WEBSITES

Apple Mobile Computing for Education: www.apple.com/education/teachers-professors/mobile-learning.html
Bretford: www.bretford.com
Datamation systems: www.pc-security.com
Promethean: http://prometheanlearning.com/us/index.php
SMART Technologies, Inc.: www.smarttech.com
Spectrum Industries: www.spectrumfurniture.com

Town School for Boys, Laptop Learning: townschool.com/technology/laptop
_program.php

NOTES

1. Saul Rockman, "A Study in Learning," *Technology & Learning* 25, no. 3 (2004): 34.

2. Domenic Grignano, "12 Tips for Launching a Wireless Laptop Program," *Technology & Learning* 25, no. 3 (2004): 37–40.

3. Rockman, "A Study in Learning," 37.

4. Tom Reardon, "Interactive Whiteboards in School: Effective Uses," *Media & Methods* 38, no. 7 (2002): 12.

5. Julie-Ann Edwards, Mike Hartnell, and Rosalind Martin, "Interactive Whiteboards: Some Lessons from the Classroom," *Micromath* 18, no. 2 (2002): 30.

6. Phil Mackall, "Interactive Whiteboards Enhance the Learning Experience for Deaf, Hard-of-Hearing Students," *T.H.E. Journal* 31, no. 10 (2004): 64.

7. Kristen Vassos, "Classroom Instruction with Electronic Whiteboards," *Media & Methods* 41, no. 2 (2004): 20.

4

TECHNOLOGY ADMINISTRATION IN THE SCHOOL LIBRARY

9

Automation

Part 4 delves into technology administration in the school library. Choices made here require a school librarian to understand the variety in technology to determine the best use of funds to meet the needs of their specific school. There's seldom a one-size-fits-all solution. Instead, the multitude of choices has made it even more complicated.

School librarians, as administrators as well as information specialists and teachers, have to make decisions that affect the day-to-day activities of how the library works and what's used to produce an efficient library for students and teachers. These decisions include the type of automation system, management of student computers, security systems, and long-range technology plans for future growth. This is a crucial role for the librarian. As experts in the field, librarians are best suited to make these decisions. This first chapter, focusing on automation systems, describes features to consider and what to look for in a vendor.

Automation in school libraries has become commonplace as the technology has improved and prices for hardware, software, and supporting items, such as barcode scanners, have become more affordable. Although software features have become standardized, there are still many vendors and products to choose from and factors to take into consideration. Decisions have therefore become ever more complicated over time. A few major names in the library automation business have garnered a good share of the market, but they're certainly not alone. Because school libraries usually have a relatively small staff with less money and time to devote to cataloging and utilizing automation system features, a relatively low-cost, simple package that's easy to learn and use is important.

What precisely is an automated library system? An automation system is most simply a computer program that contains item and patron records so that librarians can track the collection and see who has specific books checked out. It's a database with specific fields for each item that can create relationships between each record. This replaces the old-fashioned card catalog and a related system for filing physical paper cards that correlate items checked out to specific students. Although just about anyone could create their own automated system from scratch with database software, the time and effort involved to do so makes an off-the-shelf system an easy choice.

When we speak of automation, there's an implied time and cost savings that's true to some degree. Because school libraries have a relatively small student body compared to large colleges or large public libraries, the cost and time savings might not be as evident, although it's still a factor to a certain extent. Checking out books electronically is faster, and an electronic system replacing card catalogs reduces duplicate work. The largest benefit is for students in terms of being able to easily search for books. Many other benefits are discussed throughout this chapter. The chapter begins with some background information on automation systems, presents some of the factors to consider in determining your needs, discusses information on specific system features, and then concludes with some information on funding and planning.

BACKGROUND

Automation systems have been around for much longer than many of us may realize, but that's because early-adopter systems, like much in computer technology, were expensive, rare, and first implemented in only the largest institutional libraries. The University of Texas at Austin was one of the first, in the mid-1930s, to implement a library automation system. Although it was based on a punch-card system for circulation and was therefore not very user friendly, it did demonstrate future possibilities. These systems were first developed in-house and required programming staff to fully create and maintain. It wasn't until 1971 that CLSI (Computer Library Services Inc.) created the first turnkey circulation system that introduced an off-the-shelf and relatively easy-to-adopt system. CLSI was followed by DRA (Data Research Associates) shortly thereafter and several other vendors who began to realize the potential of this market.

Text-based DOS automation systems of the 1980s and early 1990s were still cumbersome to use compared to today's Windows-based systems, yet they allowed staff and students to be trained to use the software and become fully functional in their use without requiring programmers or computer staff. Use of the system was no longer just the domain of professionals; it became visible to everyday users.

Today, library automation is considered a mature technology, meaning that its widespread adoption and ease of use has created a certain degree of uniformity between different products and vendors. Certain key functionalities and basic features can now be found in almost every product. Although some very inexpensive programs will always lag in features and some very expensive programs will continue to push the boundaries, the majority of automation systems now include the same core features. These usually include authority records, bibliographic records, copy records, item records, patron records, and Z39.50 protocol (Information Retrieval Service Definition and Protocol Specifications for Library Applications). These systems will include a cataloging module for creating item records, a circulation module that links patron records to those item records, and a public access catalog so that students can search for items the library owns. Certain areas, usually in the behind-the-scenes technical services arena, have seemed to lag a bit and might contain a bit more variation. These include serials control and acquisitions processing.[1]

There's also been a marked shift in approaching automation systems at the district versus the school level. You can still purchase a system that will run from a personal computer in the library, but networked systems that provide cost savings by using a single server have become increasingly popular.

DETERMINING YOUR NEEDS

One of the first questions to ask about when considering automation systems is what is already in place and what are the needs. If your school library has never been automated, then your choice of options is pretty wide open. If you have an existing system, you need to decide at what point a change needs to take place. Some older systems have been around for so long that the vendors don't exist or, if they do, they might not support the software, don't have any updates, or can't help in terms of maintenance or problems. It can be very easy to stick with a tried-and-true system long after its usefulness has been passed. This is especially true if the library budget is small, if you don't have much technical support, and if the computers are so old that they can't even run today's demanding software. Your choices then range from finding out if upgrades are available or newer products would be easier to switch to. Staying with a current vendor ensures a better chance that upgrades and compatibility issues will cause fewer problems. However, sometimes you're better off finding a new vendor. This would require a retrospective conversion, whereby your old database of records is migrated to a new system. To ensure the smoothest transition, you should talk with the vendor and describe exactly what you have used in the past to see if they're familiar with the product. Today, this has become less and less of a problem with standardization, but very old systems could cause some problems to arise. A worst-case scenario would require an entirely new database of records to be built. Oftentimes it's more a matter of moving one set of records into the new system and then double-checking the records for any problems with the conversion, cleaning them up as necessary.

Another major decision to consider up front is whether or not your library will be on its own on a stand-alone system or if you'll be part of a district or larger system. The benefit of having a system for only your school library is that the decisions are almost entirely up to you. You don't have to worry about building a consensus with other librarians. It also means that it'll be housed locally and you'll more likely have control over upkeep, maintenance, backups, and other instances in which you might want physical access to the hardware and software. It'll probably also mean that you can use a smaller and simpler package because the requirements for the number of holdings and the number of access points will be much smaller. You'll have much more control over cataloging and the records.

On the other hand, a district-wide automation system is very appealing and has become extremely common. You do have to give up some of the control over decision making because it's a group purchase. However, it's often less expensive, saves time and money for maintenance, and allows several librarians to share expertise and training. Most importantly, it'll provide a union catalog for your district in which multiple schools and libraries can see what books and materials the others own, allowing easier resource sharing. Students moving through the district and up grade levels will have an easier time by not having to learn a new interface. Some larger urban districts can conceivably save a lot of time with cataloging records once and then only having to attach local copy information.

Recent opportunities in automation technology have provided additional choices. One of these is choosing between a local solution and an application service provider (ASP) option. Because almost every school now has Internet access, ASPs appear attractive. Instead of having to purchase, maintain, upgrade, and physically handle a local server; physically backup files; and physically load and upgrade software, an ASP handles all of that for you. All of your cataloging and patron records are entered via a password-protected website, and then any student or teacher can access the catalog from any Internet-connected computer. This makes library, classroom, and home access very simple. Smaller schools that don't have the technical support or the one-time funds to purchase everything needed for a local system have found this a great opportunity. However, like database subscriptions, this becomes a permanent monthly cost. If you decide to switch to another vendor, your time and effort might have little to no impact on students, depending on the specific contract you have previously arranged.

Furthermore, if the ASP goes out of business, you will have nothing. There are, therefore, both advantages and disadvantages.

The current trend is looking up for ASP systems and will most likely continue to grow. Although cost is a major part of the decision, local technical skills are often the driving factor. Some librarians don't feel as comfortable being in charge of so much if they're on their own. Smaller and rural schools are more likely to find this option attractive, although any school could easily choose this option.

Although it can be difficult to predict the future accurately, there's some widespread chatter that the ASP model will likely increase. We've already become used to paying for database and full-text article subscriptions, online reference-material subscriptions, reviews of kid-friendly website databases, and even downloaded video and audio clips. With fast Internet access becoming common, more and more will be done online.

Another option that smaller schools could choose if they don't have as much money is an open-source solution. Not having to purchase automation software and regular upgrades can be an exciting advantage. However, this will also mean that there's no maintenance or support desk to contact. This is not for the faint of heart. You'll need to be a bit more comfortable with technology and will have to rely on discussion boards and colleagues for answers and assistance. As more and more open-source software is utilized in other areas of the school, this option will also improve over time.

The shift to an automated library system places the school librarian in greater managerial roles. With the ease with which copy cataloging can be accomplished, most of this can be done by staff that you train. Staff can be trained to efficiently circulate items, track serials, and handle interlibrary loans. So instead of the professional librarian doing all of the cataloging and other tasks, much of this is relegated to trained staff. Your task will be to determine and oversee the system chosen; ensure that it's implemented and functioning; and then train staff, students, and teachers how to use the system depending on their needs. There's really no reduction in the number of staff you need because tasks have merely moved from one realm to another, but it does mean that more and more can be accomplished.

SYSTEMS

Automation systems are separate packages of software that contain distinct modules to pick and choose from. They work in unison and provide a common environment and interface. Certain modules are clearly more important than others. Depending on the vendor, there may be a cost savings in purchasing more modules. Some vendors might not give you as many choices, instead including certain modules together, but you need to be

aware of your options when making these decisions. Some initial considerations when reviewing vendor software include the following:

- Hardware requirements
- Support agreements
- Training
- Reports available
- Data conversion
- Z 39.50 compatibility
- Creation of new categories of nonprint items (laptops, PDAs, etc.)
- Number of simultaneous users
- Total cost

Cataloging

The most important module is cataloging. Without cataloging, there's
nothing else you can really do. This is where your books and other material
records are stored. Basic features usually include the ability to do your own
original cataloging, editing, copying, saving, and retrieving cataloged records. Most cataloging is done for you with a purchase from book vendors.
Copy cataloging handles most of the rest. The few items that you have to
do yourself complete the process. This collection of records is the heart and
soul of the system and is considered an electronic version of the shelf list
card file. A few other important considerations include the following:

- Importing of MARC records
- Cataloging of websites
- Support for merging of records from existing system

Circulation

The next most important module is circulation. This is the patron database, and it allows you to make connections between patrons and materials.
Instead of having to track book cards, the system will quickly match the two
records (patron and item). Basic features usually include material check-in
and checkout, inventory control, production and printing of overdue notices,
placement of holds for students requesting an item already checked out, recognition of reserve materials, recording of fines for overdue materials, and
statistical reports. Additional features to ask about include the following:

- Password protection for overriding system
- Internal calendar for recalculating checkout periods because of holi-
  days

- Allow patron records to be imported from other databases
- Audible error alert
- Blocking features when checkout limit is reached

Online Catalog

The online catalog is the final most important module of the system. Sometimes referred to as the OPAC (online public access catalog), Web PAC in today's environment, or simply the catalog, it's the electronic version of the public card catalog. One of the main benefits of the online catalog is the ability for students, teachers, and librarians to search using Boolean operators and with additional limits beyond the simple title, author, and subject searches. Although a simple search can still be performed, more sophisticated searches can be conducted very quickly. Furthermore, instead of a single physical point of access, patrons can access the online catalog from multiple computers in the library and from around the school. Therefore, there's less standing in line, and the process of searching can be much more efficient. If the online catalog is Web accessible, then it can be searched from home as well. Finally, another benefit of the system is that the catalog can display shelf status. Unlike a card catalog, where the patron would go to the shelf to find a book and hope that it was there, the online catalog can instantly show whether the book is checked out or not. Be sure to check on the following features:

- Searches by author, title, subject, barcode number, call number, ISBN, and combination
- Supports truncation and wildcard characters
- Features both simple and advanced search interfaces
- Makes use of stop words
- Uses built-in spell-check for finding closest match if no records found
- Allows searching with mouse or keyboard

Serials

Another useful module is serials control. Although serials modules aren't uniformly purchased because of tight budgets, they can be very useful for larger libraries that have to track many subscriptions. Smaller libraries usually choose some type of paper-based system for record keeping or some type of home-grown spreadsheet file. These can easily track when issues arrive, if issues are missing, and when it's time to renew. You can also easily track how prices increase over the years and how much you're spending. A Web page can be created to at least list the titles that are currently subscribed to. As collections grow in size, the need for better organization becomes more important. Basic features for a serials control module usually include a place to store periodical subscription information, acquisitions, routing lists, claims reports, subscriptions that have been canceled, budgeting calculations and projections, charting of vendor performance, and overall record keeping.

Acquisitions

An acquisitions module for nonserial purchases is also very handy. Although the process is simpler because of the one-time nature of each purchase, it's still important for record keeping and to ensure that all orders have been filled properly. Some type of physical folder of paperwork alongside a spreadsheet is often adequate for a smaller library. Many vendors also include some type of online material ordering. However, tracking all purchases in one place, separate from the vendors' lists, is still good practice, instead of relying entirely on a vendor website. Furthermore, for audits, budgeting, and planning, you need to track everything that you purchase. If your library is larger, you might want to consider this type of module. Standard features usually include tracking of material requests, purchase orders, material receipts, budget planning, vendor performance tracking, and overall record keeping.

Interlibrary Loan

A final module to consider is interlibrary loan. Again, record keeping is often already a combination of paper files, spreadsheets, and built into electronic systems, such as OCLC (Online Computer Library). Some type of data recording for the purpose of statistics, keeping track of costs involved, and budget planning is important, yet again for a smaller library and especially for the lower grades might not be utilized that frequently. Remember that teachers, administrators, and yourself may make use of interlibrary loan, so it could still add up to more than you think. The growing number of full-text databases can, in many instances, decrease the amount of interlibrary loan that you use, but the use of citation databases will only make it increase. Nonetheless, unless you see a heavier-than-average use, you might not need a feature-rich module like this.

Recent advancements in automation have led to what many have termed the integrated library system, which takes automation one step further. If you don't have an integrated library system now, you will before long. This is the future of library systems, and it makes sense, considering the abundance of information types. Instead of just searching for books, DVDs, CDs, and other physical materials on your library shelves, you'll be able to search for websites and through your subscription databases.[2]

This one-interface approach allows students to retrieve information on a specific subject regardless of the format of the material. Instead of having to go to multiple searches or having to repeat the search in various places, the results of one search would bring up a list of books, articles, websites, and other types of information. This is one-stop shopping. Furthermore, integrating the search to include a subscription database to kid-friendly, safe websites will only encourage students to use the libraries resources instead of venturing off onto the Web for materials that may be of questionable value.

ADDITIONAL EQUIPMENT AND MATERIALS

Purchasing the hardware and software for the automation system is the biggest and most expensive decision. There is, of course, additional equipment and materials that you'll need to fully implement automation. First are the barcodes and a barcode scanner. In the early days of personal computer–based library automation, in a DOS environment, librarians and staff had to type in the call numbers on books to bring up the record. This was extremely time-consuming, and one little mistake would bring up an error or an incorrect item. Barcodes have been the solution and prices have dropped so dramatically that it's almost unheard of to decide not to barcode a collection. For only a couple hundred dollars for the barcode scanner and pennies per barcode, the price is a relatively small piece of an entire automation project.

Barcode scanners come in many forms. Wand type scanners are usually less expensive and require the user to drag the tip over the barcode label. This has a tendency to degrade the barcode over time because of the physical contact generated between the device and the barcode, and the tip is prone to damage. However, in a low-circulating collection, this might have little impact. The preferred system is a CCD (charged-couple device) gun-type scanner that can either be handheld or placed in a mounting stand. The barcode is then simply placed a couple inches below the scanner and the laser light reflected back reads the code. These scanners vary considerably in terms of how they read the barcodes, so be sure to read all of the specifications. Some models can be held eight inches away from the barcode while others need to be almost touching.

A portable scanner for inventory purposes is a popular option. Simply carry the scanner and scan every book on the shelf in a single day or two. Then you can plug the scanner into the computer and compare what is on the shelf to what the catalog shows. Lost and stolen item lists can be instantly generated for the purposes ranging from cleaning up the database to determining what items need to be bought again.

JAMES C. KIRKPATRICK LIBRARY - CMSU

3 7250 04023535 8

Figure 9.1.   Codabar

The barcode labels themselves are relatively inexpensive, although bar-coding an entire library that has never been done before can add up to a few hundred dollars. While most vendors will provide information on standard barcode labels, there are competing styles. The most common in the library world is the 14-digit Codabar. The first digit identifies whether it's a patron or item, the next four provide a unique library ID, the next eight provide a unique ID (whether patron or item), and the last digit is a check digit. See figure 9.1.

A short and simple library or school name should be included on the label so that parents and students can easily identify where the book is from—even if they don't look for other markings or stamps. The school ID number is not chosen randomly but instead should be coordinated through the state library system so that you aren't using someone else's code. Although this probably wouldn't cause a problem, conflicts are possible, and you don't want to have to recode an entire library years down the road because of an earlier mistake.

The location of the barcode on the books should be standardized so that the person at the circulation desk knows exactly where to look for it every time. Beyond that, it's up to you to decide where to place it. Some people prefer to place it on the inside of the book, front or back cover, to protect the barcode from damage when pulled off of shelves, placed on tables, or moved around. If you're planning to use your system for inventory, this doesn't work well because you would have to take each and every book off the shelf to scan. In this case, putting the barcode someplace on the outside cover would only require the book to be pulled slightly out, scanned, then quickly pushed back in. A strong and durable barcode label is important. If it's damaged too easily, it won't be read and will have to be replaced. Most barcode labels are protected by a thin film of transparent plastic. Most vendors sell different thicknesses for different prices. In most instances, a standard thickness will be more than enough. If you're concerned about a heavy-use item, an additional piece of strong transparent book tape could be placed over the barcode to protect it further.

Barcodes for patrons is a slightly different situation because of the variability between schools. For younger students who might not be expected to carry and keep track of a library card, a possible solution is to keep a three-ring binder of note cards for each class at the circulation desk. Each note card has a student name and barcode affixed to it. Then the person at the circulation desk can fairly quickly find the student barcode and scan it in. Older students should be able to keep their own cards. The question is whether the library wants to purchase cards from a vendor or if the school utilizes an ID system. If there is an existing ID system, then coordination between school, library, and card vendors could make one card work for everything needed.

Automation systems also work in concert with security systems. At point of checkout and check-in, materials should be sensitized and desensitized. More information about security system products is included in a later chapter.

Finally, new advances in technology provide more options than ever before. Some libraries are moving ahead with RFID (radio frequency identification) chips in place of barcodes. The convenience here is that the RFID scanner only needs to come near the item for it to be recognized instead of a clear and concise laser scan. It might not circulate books faster, but it could speed up the inventory process. Because RFID chips are dropping in price from increased levels of use in business and industry, it's hoped that this could translate into saving for libraries down the road. By using the same chips and readers used elsewhere, it becomes an inexpensive off-the-shelf technology. This is what has happened with barcodes and scanners. Libraries weren't the first and only users of barcodes, but worldwide acceptance has made them more affordable. If RFID systems take off as expected, prices will be lower for libraries as well.

There are some concerns that someone with a reader could find out what you are carrying down the street. However, the fact that the chip will contain only a number that correlates to the bibliographic record of the item in the database will not be of much help to anyone else. Also, some are concerned that in the future these chips could contain more information than that, but this is not the plan now.

FUNDING AND PLANNING

Automating a library isn't cheap, but it isn't rare and expensive either. Prices have come down so that it's a reasonable and common expectation for all school libraries, but there are definite one-time costs and ongoing costs to budget for.[3] Initially, there are costs for hardware, software, barcode scanners, utilities, and supplies, such as barcodes. Money also needs to be set aside for training, personnel, maintenance and support for the software, additional barcode labels, and eventual replacement as hardware needs to be upgraded. Grant money can help in this process, and one-time money from the school will also help to get a project of this size moving. However, continual support in the form of the library budget must be calculated and supported by the administration. This should be done through ongoing technology planning.

Planning for an automation project isn't simple, but it's straightforward. You need to expect the project to take over a year, with a great deal of pre-planning and preparation. Beyond the decision of choosing a vendor and purchasing hardware and software, there are additional steps that need to take place and items for consideration. For instance, any time that you're about to make a major change in the library in terms of automation is the time to do a thorough weeding. Whether this will be a new system or a conversion to new software, don't take the time to process an item that you don't want. Get rid of those materials first and it will mean less records to deal with later.

This is also a good time to clean up the records. Look for and correct records with misspelled words, incorrect or awkward subject headings, and other errors. Don't let past errors propagate into the new system. This is the time to clean it up.

Plan for how you want to back up files with the new automation system. Don't wait until the system crashes and all of the work needs to be done again. Make a plan and put procedures into place from day one. If the system is from an ASP or is implemented at the district level, you might not have to personally back up files, but do find out what they do. If you do the backup yourself, determine how frequently to do the backup and therefore how much you are willing to lose if you don't follow through, as well as the backup medium. This could range from rewritable CDs to a USB flash drive. Regardless of what you choose, be sure to have more than just one backup, so that you can go back to a prior backup if something happened to the last one. Having three or four backups is good practice. It's also a good idea to test it and see if the backup works. Early on, use one of the backup disks and test it. See if it works properly. Finally, be sure that you keep the backup in a secure and safe place. Don't leave it next to the server where, if the building were to flood, the backup would be destroyed along with the server.

Training for staff is another important consideration. Don't wait until after frustrations have started to finally start thinking about training. When choosing a vendor, determine if they have training available and how much it costs. Sometimes the librarian can go to a training session in a "train the trainer" approach, whereby the librarian passes the information along to staff instead of paying for costly sessions for everyone. It's also a good idea to be sure that any training materials, documentation, manuals, and websites are kept available and free for everyone to use. Librarians and staff may want to start perusing these materials ahead of time, before any formal training occurs. Then when training does occur, you can focus on the basic features that they'll use more often before getting to advanced features.

As you're thinking about training staff, remember that students and teachers will need instruction as well. Nothing is more frustrating for a student than walking into a library and seeing that the system has changed and not knowing where to start. Provide handouts, instructions, and cheat sheets by the computers, and distribute them to teachers and classes. Use library time to offer lessons in using the new system, and vary them depending on age level and what you expect of the students. This is also a good opportunity for professional development for teachers so that they're aware of the changes in the library. Take the opportunity to publicize the library and let everyone know about the positive changes and what the library can offer. This is a good way to get free PR and to showcase all of your work and your importance to the curriculum. This can be a springboard for future collaboration.

The concept of basic library lessons can't be underestimated. Keep in mind that this can be more than simply showing students a new automation system. It can lead into a lesson on the new features available, lessons about Boolean operators, and lessons on library research and information literacy. A change, whether a new system or an upgrade, can become the cornerstone of a set of library lessons that gets students into the library.

In terms of planning, don't forget to do more than just talk to a few vendors by yourself. While much more will probably be done automatically as part of a district purchase, whether you are on your own or part of a district, you want to include as many people as possible in the decision. This is a major purchase for the library and will have implications for years to come. Be sure that the principal and other librarians and staff are involved in the process. Whether or not you have to complete official RFPs (request for proposals) for your school, ensure that you have all of the information you can get from the websites of the vendors you're considering and search the literature, e-mail lists, and websites in general for any positive or negative information you can find. You should feel comfortable calling and talking to vendors not only for the information but also to see if they're available and helpful. Finally, talk to other librarians in the area and in your part of the state. Find out what everyone else is using and how happy they are with what they have.

Whether the automation system is new or upgraded, this is also the time to consider requirements for how it interacts with the rest of the library. Is the current circulation desk satisfactory? Do you need new wiring? How many OPAC computers do your students need? For any of the computers, student or library, have the system requirements increased so high that current computers can't handle running the software? Where do you plan on cataloging? You should have at least one computer for circulation and another for cataloging. Do you need new or more printers? You should have a printer at the circulation computer, and a printer should also be available for students. The ratio of student computers to printers depends on the activities you expect at those stations. At a minimum, you'll also need scrap paper and pencils for students to write down call numbers. All of these types of questions need to be planned before rather than after.

A final consideration while evaluating automation systems is the type of reports that can be generated. For example, an age report can easily and instantly provide statistics on how old your collection is in certain subject areas, how that compares to what your state requires for school certification standards, and in general what your strengths and weaknesses are in the collection. This is helpful not only for yourself for collection development but also when providing the hard numbers that your principal needs for the library budget. Many types of information can be generated that could never realistically be done prior to automation. Make use of the data to better serve the students.

WEBSITES

Library Technology Guides: www.librarytechnology.org

VENDORS

Alexandria: www.goalexandria.com
Auto-Graphics, Inc.: www4.auto-graphics.com
Book Systems, Inc.: www.booksys.com
Eloquent Systems, Inc.: www.eloquent-systems.com
EOS International: www.eosintl.com
Follett: www.follettsoftware.com/
Innovative Interfaces: www.iii.com
Koha–Open source library system: www.koha.org
LearningAccess ILS–Open Source Integrated Library System: www.learning
   access.org/tools/ils.php
LibraryWorld: www.libraryworld.com
Mandarin: www.mlasolutions.com
SirsiDynix: www.sirsidynix.com/
Surpass: www.surpasssoftware.com

NOTES

1. Thomas R. Kochtanek and Joseph R. Matthews, *Library Information Systems: From Library Automation to Distributed Information Access Solutions* (Westport, CT: Libraries Unlimited, 2002), 17.

2. Walter Minkel, "A Smarter System," *School Library Journal* 49, no. 11 (November 2003): 48.

3. Dania Bilal, *Automating Media Centers and Small Libraries* (Greenwood Village, CO: Libraries Unlimited, 2002), 24.

10

Student Computers

This chapter shifts to looking closer at computer decisions and issues surrounding administration and oversight of library student computers. Although we've already covered some of the basic hardware and software configurations and the importance of security software such as antivirus, spyware, and firewalls, there are additional considerations to keep in mind when maintaining multiuser library computers. This chapter presents information on replacing and maintaining computers for everyday use, as well as securing them physically and preventing damage to their software systems.

One of the hardest issues with student computers is basic maintenance and keeping them working and up-to-date. Your own computer, whether it's at work or at home, is much easier to keep track of because you use it every day. You know exactly when something breaks or doesn't work right because it immediately affects your use. You know when updates and plug-ins are installed because of prompts and alerts or because of diligence in checking your own software. When it comes to public-use computers, someone has to take responsibility for similar actions. Problems occur when no one feels responsible and therefore no one takes responsibility. Over the span of a school year, computers can fall into disarray without continued oversight.

Whether or not you have technical support and regardless of the degree of that support, you're the first line of defense for library computers. The students will look to you first when problems occur or when they have questions. Issues with library computers will directly impact your workday and how effective student learning in the library is. You need to be proactive instead of simply waiting for students to come to you with problems. The more computers that you have to maintain, the more difficult this can be.

You need to spend time to periodically check each computer to be sure all software is up-to-date, patched, and working properly. It's also a good idea to physically check the hardware for damage or problems before they escalate into something more. Additional tasks include listening for proper fan movement and feeling for a breeze at the outlets; opening and closing the CD/DVD bays; cleaning the mice, monitors, and keyboards; and ensuring that monitors and towers are still placed where they're supposed to be.

NUMBER AND ARRANGEMENT OF COMPUTERS

The number of student computers available in the library needs to be based on many different factors. Money is, of course, always a big issue, not just for the initial purchase, but also for continued maintenance and replacements. The number of computers and their arrangement will affect how your students utilize the library and the way that lessons can be completed. Even though more and more classrooms have computers in them, computer labs are built for classrooms to utilize, and mobile labs help to provide additional computer access to students, you'll still need computers within the physical library itself. It's a judgment call as to whether some computers will be dedicated to certain functions, such as the online catalog, databases, Web searching, multimedia, or educational software and other programs, such as Accelerated Reader. It also depends on if there's an adjoining or entirely incorporated computer lab with the library. Regardless, you need to have some way that you can work with entire classes, as opposed to just one or two students at a time. Whether this means one computer per student or some doubling up often depends on money and space constraints, unless you're lucky enough to be involved with a new building construction.

The number of computers to maintain should ideally be part of an ongoing technology plan, as opposed to being pieced together in a random fashion when money is found. Although this is still sometimes the case, you won't want to turn down surprise gifts. Even if a rotation plan is in place where computers are shifted from one school or area to another based on age, you should still have some type of plan and rationale for what you need in your library. Some schools, districts, and states have formulas to follow. For instance, in the *Standards for Missouri School Library Media Centers*, three levels of computer workstations are described. The first level states that the library should have workstations equal to one-third of the average class size. Level two proposes having one-half of the average class enrollment, meaning that an average class would double up on computers for a lesson in the library. The goal is to reach the third level, in which there exists a one-to-one relationship, meaning there are as many computers as the average class size.[1]

Of course, once you purchase or obtain a computer, it's really a temporary device. When you speak of a computer lasting years (as opposed to days or weeks), it might not feel like a temporary device, but the life cycle of a computer is still relatively short compared to furniture and other items in a school. Although the software needs to be updated continually for compatibility and safety issues, computers only last so long. Some districts have a rotation cycle in place, whereby older computers are passed down from more heavily used areas to lesser-used areas and areas where the software requirements aren't as strict. This happens in business, higher education, and often in our homes. Many parents pass down computers to the kids when they buy a new one. This isn't always a bad thing, but it does place restrictions on usability.

Some districts and schools place specific numbers on the life cycle of computers. For instance, in Missouri the suggested standard is to replace computers every four years. That number is a general rule in many organizations and businesses. You should expect about four years of use from a computer. Anything beyond that depends on your needs and how far you can stretch the computer's use. Although this might sound reasonable and you can easily picture the issues that come about as computers reach that age, the implications are important. To spread out purchases as well as the time involved with setting up and installing computers, you should expect to replace about one-fourth of your computers each year. That can add up to a lot of time and money. Shifting computers to lesser-used areas stretches out the life cycle, but it also means more time and energy to physically set up the computer and install the programs needed. You can only realistically shift computers so many times before the computer gets too old to do anything and before you start spending all of your time moving and setting up computers. Shifting computers once or twice is about all you want to do. Beyond that, the savings are seldom worth it.

Furthermore, it can be difficult to have different computers with different ages and hardware specifications in the same room or area. This is why classrooms, labs, and libraries tend to be upgraded all at once. So one year a lab might be upgraded, the next a couple classrooms, the next the library, and so on. The library would then be on a rotation to have all of its computers replaced every fourth year.

Consideration also needs to be made for the location and arrangement of computers in a library. This varies greatly depending on the layout of library space (i.e., whether the library is square, rectangular, round, etc.). Doors, walls, and offices have to be worked around; circulation desks and stacks might be difficult or impossible to move; and other features and safety issues could leave you with less space to play with than you originally thought. With the space that's left, you'll then need to decide if the computers will be placed against a wall (as seen in figure 10.1) or in groups, which

| Computer Desk 1 | Computer Desk 2 | Computer Desk 3 |

Figure 10.1.   Computers against a Wall

will also vary depending on the computer desks you're using (as seen in figures 10.2 and 10.3).

Another factor to consider is ergonomics. When you're taking the time to determine how many computers are needed, where to place them, and how to arrange them, you must also consider the use of the equipment from an ergonomic perspective. In a classroom or computer lab situation, part of this consideration focuses on the student being able to work on the computer and also see the teacher and teacher displays. The ability to have the least amount of twisting and turning is ideal, especially if a great deal of time will be spent in such activities. This can be difficult when you're trying to accomplish multiple activities in the same room. In those cases, a flexible laptop structure would ease some of this difficulty. Although laptops in the library can certainly be initiated, wired computers and fixed desks are still the norm.

Other ergonomic considerations include the physical size of the desks and chairs, how easily students can reach the keyboard and mouse, and how easily they can see the monitor. Much of the literature already guides

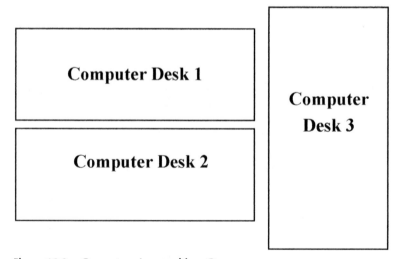

Figure 10.2.   Computers Arranged in a Group

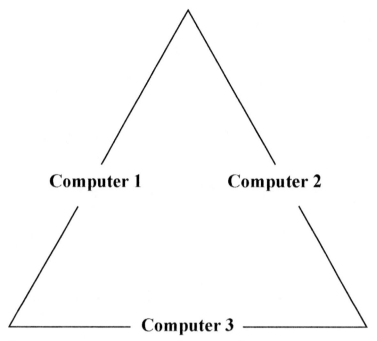

Figure 10.3. Computers Arranged in a Triangular Group

some of these decisions, and some states like Missouri have specific guidelines. For instance, in terms of seating it's recommended that there should be knee space at least 27 inches high, 30 inches wide, and 19 inches deep. The computer work surfaces should be from 28 to 34 inches from the floor. Minimum clear aisle space at traditional card catalogs, magazine displays, or reference stacks should be a minimum of 36 inches. Maximum reach height should be 48 inches, irrespective of forward or side reach allowed.[2]

The basic principle with ergonomics is that students should have appropriate furniture for their size. This is usually already done in the classroom to some degree. Children do vary greatly in size, and at least some consideration of desk and chair sizes is taken into account for different grade levels and schools. Computers in the schools are relatively newer, at least when compared to other school furniture. It's easy to forget that what works for us as adults won't work well for kids. Adjustable chairs are ideal, but more expensive. At a minimum, be sure that students can reach the keyboards and mice without stretching and that they can see the monitor without having to look up high.

Another concern with computers in the library is their physical security. Although computers and monitors are unlikely to walk off by themselves during the school day, we do have to understand that the building is often open for many other hours throughout the week. Depending on the layout of the school, this might mean that there are no library doors to lock, and the library could be unsupervised. With the increasing use of thin LCDs, it's becoming easier for individuals to take equipment in backpacks or other bags. For some schools, this might never really be a concern. However, if theft is a possibility, then a simple security cable with locks is an inexpensive measure. Be sure to lock the monitor and the central processing unit to the table. Although even these cables can be cut and there's never a fail-safe method of preventing theft, they'll eliminate all but the most serious of criminals.

Librarians and teachers have discovered smaller security issues that must be dealt with. For instance, as mentioned earlier, students have a tendency to remove the balls found in older computer mice. This may not be the biggest issue in libraries today, but it can cause a great deal of frustration for library users. Don't make the mistake of gluing the cover closed because you won't be able to open it for cleaning. An unclean mouse will be unusable before the life expectancy expires. Therefore, the solution today is to purchase optical mice. Even though optical mice are more expensive than the older mice with track balls, they're well worth it. Keep these issues in mind as students tend to do anything they can get away with. It depends on the location of the computers and how visible they are to librarians and staff and others in the school, but you might choose to lock computer cases, place locks on drives, and position computers so that students cannot unplug or power off computers.

You shouldn't have to open the PC (personal computer) case frequently, but you might have to remove stuck disks. This was more of a problem with $3\frac{1}{2}$-inch floppy disks because of the moving parts that protect the internal surface. CDs and DVDs can also get stuck by completely innocent students. A simple computer tool kit with small pliers and tweezers, screwdrivers, and other devices is invaluable for instant hardware troubleshooting when time is important and you can't wait for other technical support.

Finally, food and drinks in the library can also cause problems with equipment. While most K–12 libraries don't allow food and drinks, some allow it on special occasions and events; all it takes is one instance to make you think about what can happen. Realistically, however, unless you have a very awkward arrangement of computers and desks, spills tend to fall directly on keyboards and mice instead of the more expensive computer. Vacuuming can remove crumbs, but it can be difficult to get sticky keys and mice unstuck. The best thing to do is to unplug the equipment and take it apart. The keys on the keyboard can be taken off one by one and cleaned with a damp cloth, and mice can usually be unscrewed and taken apart also. Luckily, prices have come down so much that if you can't get it working again, it won't be much of a problem to replace. Furthermore, people today are more cognizant of food and drink issues around computers than they were 15–20 years ago. You don't see the dust covers placed over keyboards every night any longer, and less damage occurs than we worry about. So keep an eye on food and drinks, but don't stress too much. Most likely, the biggest expense will be a $20 keyboard if accidents do occur.

Software use is an additional concern on public-access computers. Regardless of the amount of desktop security you utilize or the status of filters while searching the Internet, some activities need to be governed, and decisions regarding these activities can be made solely within the library or within the larger school or district. For instance, you should have a policy on the use of computer games. On the one hand, a harmless game of solitaire or other simple noneducational game might be viewed as perfectly acceptable for students who are done with their work. Or there could be fears that even these games can get out of hand and in the way of what students should be doing. Furthermore, if computers are scarce and students often have to wait in line for availability, then you don't want to have to monitor students to be sure that what they're doing is legitimate. Therefore, a policy needs to be in place and games need to either be allowed or deleted.

Whether or not games are allowed, students may also try to download games, programs, or other items like music. Here, too, a policy needs to be set. It can be difficult to block some of these activities without getting in the way of legitimate work. This is also true of such activities as e-mail. Some schools worry about privacy and safety issues and want to block students from using e-mail. However, there can be legitimate uses of this as well, and policies regarding e-mail will impact librarian and teacher use of computers also. Here, too, a policy needs to be developed. Although e-mail has been largely prohibited or blocked in the past, there's a rising realization of how important and useful it is. Many schools now supply students with e-mail accounts. However, some districts have been known to block free e-mail accounts other than the official school accounts. Hotmail, Gmail, and others can be individually blocked.

DESKTOP SECURITY

As just mentioned, several issues can impact desktop and network security as well as safety. On the one hand, we want computers to be open and available for students to do everything that they need to learn. Indeed, the National Educational Technology Standards expect students to become comfortable with using technology, and locking them out from everything but the barest essentials is not productive.[3]

Securing the software on library computers takes more than simple oversight because you can't stand over students' shoulders as they work. Although this would be a wonderful solution, at least to teachers and librarians, budgets don't allow for that kind of increase in staff. Maintaining antivirus, antispam, and login rights; updating the operating system with patches; and keeping up with current software is a bare minimum. However, that won't keep students from changing settings and deleting crucial files. The two approaches to protecting student computers from students are by preventing them from making changes and by undoing what they've done.

In order to prevent students from making changes on the computer, whether intentionally or unintentionally, that will have repercussions for other users, the most direct method is to simply lock students out from specific functions and features. Products from Fortres and Faronics allow those with administrative computer rights, via a password-protected system, to decide what students have access to. This could include anything from blocking downloads to preventing installation of software to blocking access to file directories, computer settings, or specific menu items. This will stop the devious student who wants to see what they can get into and it will also help the student who's afraid of breaking the computer by knowing it's not possible to accidentally delete important files. The drawbacks to these solutions is that a too restrictive setting will lock out students from valid activities and also that it might not give students the opportunity to work on a computer that functions exactly like what they have at home. However, these security programs have a great deal of flexibility, and you can turn feature settings on and off, depending on your own preferences and comfort level.

An open-source alternative is Open Kiosk. This program is designed for schools and libraries and is meant to keep students out of areas in the computer where librarians don't want the students to interfere.

Another solution is to easily undo what students have done by using programs like Clean Slate from Fortres and Deep Freeze from Faronics. With these programs, the computer reverts to the original setting when the student logs out. This way, any changes that the student has made will be undone. As an administrator, you'd have password access to update and change the computer and keep those changes intact. In effect, it's an undo feature. Whatever the student has done, whether minor or major, will be undone the next time someone logs in, and the computer will be as good as new.

Another useful tool is Symantec Ghost. Ghost software, regardless of vendor, allows you (or whoever's overseeing the computers) to set up a single computer with everything you need installed on it and all of the settings adjusted to your own preferences—everything from operating system to browsers to other software. That single image can then be copied onto other computers with ease. The benefit is that if you have a room of 20 computers, you don't have to install each program on 20 computers, adjust settings, and individually make each and every change 20 times. Instead, you just set up the one computer, and then copy it onto all the rest in one fell swoop.

Finally, we need to keep in mind that a combination and variation of these programs may be needed depending on your setup. If you want a computer dedicated to the online catalog, then you might want a program like Fortres to block all other uses. You could have Clean Slate on the rest of the student computers in the library, and leave your circulation computer completely open for you and your staff. There's no one best solution.

FILTERS

Filters on library computers have been a point of contention that will most likely continue into the near future. Both sides offer valued arguments, which implies that no single solution will meet every need. The basic principle has been described with a swimming pool analogy. Do we close and lock up the swimming pools because of their danger or do we teach students how to swim with lifeguards nearby to help when needed? The problem, as with many issues on the Internet, is that no program is 100 percent perfect. Mistakes are bound to happen with 8 billion Web pages and millions added daily, many of which come and go. No filter completely protects students while simultaneously allowing them to access everything they need. It would be safer to lock up the swimming pools. It would be safer if all they had access to was the shallow wading pool. However, most of us would rather let them swim under guidance.

There are two main ways filters work. First, filters block access to specific websites that people have personally viewed and deemed unsafe, and second, keyword filters block the rest of the sites that can't be humanly reviewed. Blocked categories include text and photos of an adult sexual nature, drugs, violence and hate, racism, gambling, tobacco, alcohol, and others. Some filters may restrict outgoing information, but usually the incoming content is of most concern. Filters vary based on the vendors' individual focus and mission, so no two products precisely match. Furthermore, vendors aren't required to disclose how their product works. Filtering criteria is considered a trade secret.[4] Some vendors have their own agendas and might, for instance, block sites that deal with homosexuality or other topics that they deem controversial. The question that naturally arises, therefore, is, how exactly are librarians supposed to evaluate and use these products when they can't see exactly how and what they're blocking?

Two common filtering problems are overblocking and underblocking. In the case of overblocking, helpful and safe websites are blocked by mistake, usually because key words are mistakenly flagged because the context is not factored in by the automation process. Sites mistakenly blocked include those on Quakers, Native Americans, safe sex, AIDS prevention, some political sites, and more.[5] Health sites are especially notorious for being blocked. For example, sites on breast cancer survivors are sometimes blocked because of the word *breast.*

Underblocking is a problem if the filters give a false sense of security to teachers, students, and parents. A study done by the Kaiser Foundation[6] found that using the most restrictive settings block 91 percent of porn sites but also 24 percent of health-information sites. The least restrictive settings block 87 percent porn and only 1.4 percent health. Therefore, no system is blocking everything that librarians and teachers want blocked, and good sites will always be blocked by accident. Placing filters on the computers won't protect students; they still need support and guidance.

Filters can have surprising and unintended effects. Because of overblocking and underblocking mistakes, some proponents of filters find themselves switching sides or at least recognizing that current technology has problems. For instance, one public library was in the spotlight at a media event to show off its newly filtered computers to the press, only to discover after installation that the library home page itself was being blocked. Flesh Public Library in Piqua, Ohio, realized in a very public forum that Net Nanny blocked the library's website at www.piquaoh.org/library.htm. They had some quick scrambling to fix the problem, but it shows how easily mistakes like this can happen. How many other websites are being blocked, and their creators don't even realize that it's happening?

It's especially humorous when politicians and others have found their websites blocked. For instance, Jeffrey Pollock ran for Congress in Oregon in 2000 and was promoting federal mandates for Internet-blocking software in public schools and libraries. Unfortunately, he discovered that that his campaign site was blocked by the filters.

Although it's tempting to generalize, we should keep in mind that filtering needs to vary by type of environment. Filters on home computers are an entirely different scenario than in the school libraries, which is also different from public libraries. At home, parents might want extra safety precautions by using CyberPatrol, Net Nanny, or GuardiaNet to watch over their children when they can't. Likewise, filters are in place at the public library because librarians can't stand over the shoulders of young patrons. However, public libraries need to be able to turn the filters off easily on the request of adults. The main purpose is to protect children who are unattended. In schools, minors have a lot more guidance and oversight, with an emphasis on education and instruction on using the Web safely. An argument could be made that school libraries are the place not to use filters so that students can be fully instructed on how to safely navigate an open Web.

Several laws bind school libraries to protect our children regardless of what we teach them about Internet safety. These include CPPA, COPA, and CIPA.

CPPA (Child Pornography Prevention Act) expanded the definition of child pornography. CPPA criminalized the creation of what's called "virtual child pornography," or "morphed" child pornography. Under CPPA, images that appear to depict children but don't, including images of youthful-looking adults or computer-generated images, are illegal.

COPA (Child Online Protection Act) prohibits the transmission of any material over the Internet deemed "harmful to minors," if the communication was made for a commercial purpose. While the concept was important, challenges to the constitutional authority of this act led congress to repeal this law after 10 years.

CIPA (Children's Internet Protection Act) passed in 2000 requires libraries and schools to install filters on their Internet computers to retain federal funding and discounts for computers and computer access (E-rate) and Library Service and Technology Act grants. This was put into effect on June 30, 2004. This includes a technology protection measure that protects against access to visual depictions in specified categories: child pornography, obscenity, and material that is "harmful to minors." CIPA defines *minor* as "an individual who has not attained the age of 17."[7] Furthermore, this act also requires the institution of an Internet Safety Policy to be put into effect. Because of this, 96 percent of schools and public libraries have some type of policy in place, with the remaining schools sure to catch up soon.[8]

An interesting component of this act requires that filters be put on all computers in the school (student, staff, and administrators), regardless of whether students access those computers. Although adults in a school—because they're adults—have the authority to turn their filters off themselves, local policies may dictate who'll actually have that authority.

The American Library Association (ALA) continues to be vocal on the use of filters in libraries. On July 2, 1997, the ALA Council put forth a Resolution on the Use of Filtering Software in Libraries, which states that "the American Library Association affirms that the use of filtering software by libraries to block access to constitutionally protected speech violates the *Library Bill of Rights*" (see table 10.1). See also ALA's website for more information on Intellectual Freedom issues.

Filters are a control issue. How does the government step in and how do local policies affect library work with our students? It would seem to make sense that librarians should have control over filter settings, the option to delete and add sites and terms, and the ability to override blocked sites

Table 10.1.   Resolution on the Use of Filtering Software in Libraries

WHEREAS, On June 26, 1997, the United States Supreme Court issued a sweeping
    reaffirmation of core First Amendment principles and held that communications
    over the Internet deserve the highest level of Constitutional protection; and
WHEREAS, The Court's most fundamental holding is that communications on the
    Internet deserve the same level of Constitutional protection as books, magazines,
    newspapers, and speakers on a street corner soapbox. The Court found that the
    Internet "constitutes a vast platform from which to address and hear from a world-
    wide audience of millions of readers, viewers, researchers, and buyers," and that
    "any person with a phone line can become a town crier with a voice that resonates
    farther than it could from any soapbox"; and
WHEREAS, For libraries, the most critical holding of the Supreme Court is that libraries
    that make content available on the Internet can continue to do so with the same
    Constitutional protections that apply to the books on libraries' shelves; and
WHEREAS, The Court's conclusion that "the vast democratic flora of the Internet" merit
    full constitutional protection will also serve to protect libraries that provide their
    patrons with access to the Internet; and
WHEREAS, The Court recognized the importance of enabling individuals to receive
    speech from the entire world and to speak to the entire world. Libraries provide
    those opportunities to many who would not otherwise have them; and
WHEREAS, The Supreme Court's decision will protect that access; and
WHEREAS, The use in libraries of software filters which block Constitutionally
    protected speech is inconsistent with the United States Constitution and federal law
    and may lead to legal exposure for the library and its governing authorities; now,
    therefore, be it
RESOLVED, That the American Library Association affirms that the use of filtering
    software by libraries to block access to constitutionally protected speech violates
    the *Library Bill of Rights*.

Adopted by the ALA Council, July 2 1997

on the fly. However, many schools require a formal request to unblock a
site, requiring an administrative or tech director intervention.[9] Because this
tends to be a slow process, people tend to not bother, instead looking for
other websites that will make it past the filter. The reason for needing that
specific site a few days later might not be there. This makes administrators
think that there are no problems, only compounding the issue.

The other problem is the lack of control over the filtering software
production. Because school librarians can't build their own automation
systems, Web browsers, and other software, they rely on vendors to supply
filters. There might be some voice from ALA and library researchers, but
the average librarian has little to no say and has effectively conceded the
choices to software filter vendors.[10]

One solution is to get larger groups together to create their own filters.
This has occurred in Kansas. The Kansas State Library created their own
filter, and they provide it free of charge through a proxy server.[11] This can't

be done by individuals or even small districts, but the more that different groups work on these problems, the more options could become available down the road.

Librarians already have a long history of helping people find appropriate information. Librarians produce book lists, finding guides, and now Web pages with links to safe sites, child-safe search engines, and databases. If we don't teach students how to safely navigate the Web, then we risk their uncovering these sites when they are on an unfiltered computer at grandma's house, a friend's house, or any place else. Regardless of federal, state, and local requirements and guidelines, we need to prepare students for what's outside of our school walls.

WEBSITES

Bess Internet Filtering: www.securecomputing.com
Children and the Internet Sample Policies: www.ala.org/ala/mgrps/divs/alsc/ issuesadv/internettech/childrentheinternetpoliciesthatwork/children internetsamppol.cfm
CIPA: www.ala.org/ala/aboutala/offices/wo/woissues/civilliberties/cipaweb/ cipa.cfm
Faronics: www.faronics.com
Fortres: www.fortresgrand.com/
GetNetWise: www.getnetwise.org
Library Software Filters: http://libraryfiltering.org
Open Kiosk: http://openkiosk.sourceforge.net
Symantec Ghost: www.symantec.com/sabu/ghost

NOTES

1. Missouri Department of Elementary and Secondary Education, *Standards for Missouri School Library Media Centers*, 2002, http://dese.mo.gov/divimprove/curriculum/ standards/02standards.pdf (accessed June 3, 2006), 26.

2. Missouri Department of Elementary and Secondary Education, *School Library Media Standards Handbook*, 2003, http://dese.mo.gov/divimprove/curriculum/library (accessed June 3, 2006), 8, 13.

3. Joe Huber, "Desktop Security . . . Now More Than Ever," *Library Media Connection* 23, no. 4 (January 2005): 58.

4. Linda Koss, "Filtering Is Not the Answer," *Library Journal* 130, no. 1 (January 2005): 70.

5. Nancy Kranich, "Why Filters Won't Protect Children or Adults," *Library Administration & Management* 18, no. 1 (Winter 2004): 14.

6. Henry J. Kaiser Family Foundation, *See No Evil: How Internet Filters Affect the Search for Online Health Information,* www.kff.org/entmedia/20021210a-index.cfm (accessed April 15, 2005).

7. American Library Association, *CIPA Questions and Answers,* www.ala.org/ala/washoff/WOissues/civilliberties/cipaweb/adviceresources/CIPAQA.pdf (accessed June 3, 2006).

8. Ann Curry and Ken Haycock, "Filtered or Unfiltered?" *School Library Journal* 47, no. 1 (January 2001): 44.

9. Walter Minkel, "Who's Blocking Whom? School Librarians Have Little Say in Online Filtering Decisions," *School Library Journal* 49, no. 6 (June 2003): 35.

10. Candace Morgan, "Internet Filtering and Individual Choice," *Oregon Library Association Quarterly* 10, no. 4 (Winter 2004): 7.

11. Walter Minkel, "A Filter That Lets Good Information In," *School Library Journal* 50, no. 3 (March 2004): 28.

11

Security Systems

Theft or loss of library materials has plagued libraries from the beginning. However, you don't need to chain books to heavy tables like in the Middle Ages because technology has made it much easier and more affordable to ensure that few library materials walk off never to return. Indeed, with tight budgets an ever-present issue, librarians of all kinds need to consider how best to ensure that every penny is spent wisely. There's nothing more frustrating than taking an inventory and realizing that titles are missing.

Loss of books and other library materials, such as CDs, DVDs, videotapes, and magazines, vary widely from library to library. Different patterns and problems are found at different types of libraries—whether they be academic, public, or school—and differences can be found within those subsets, whether the school is a K–12 or a middle school. There are even differences between schools in the same district.

Librarians want people to use the collection, so there's an inherent conflict between access and security. The open nature of the school library with classes streaming in and out all day long, students individually visiting, and the limited number of staff for assistance let alone supervision only makes the task of securing books more difficult.

On top of that, many school libraries are simply not designed for security. While there may not be direct entrances and exits to the outside of the building, many school libraries are meant to be open and inviting areas, many times with multiple entrances and exits to other corridors. Sometimes they even lack certain walls, instead having no defined boundary and simply merging with hallways and other spaces. The open center-of-the-school atmosphere is enticing, but from a security standpoint it can sometimes be almost impossible to oversee.

The simplest solution is to look at the existing environment before considering technology. Although environments vary by library, easy solutions in any school might mean moving furniture and desks so that librarians and staff have a better view of students as they exit the library. Better layout could also mean that librarians can see students in the book stacks, which might make students think twice about placing a book in their backpack. Other environment modifications include closing or limiting exits, not allowing backpacks or book bags into the library so you can see what students take with them, and simply keeping a close eye on students and collections.

Several different stages of security can be followed. Some schools might find that a combination of approaches works best for them. This is sometimes referred to as the Defense-in-Depth principle.[1]

The first and simplest approach is deterrence. This is simply reminding students that library materials must be checked out before taking them home or to their classrooms. This starts with the school librarian introducing students to check-out procedures at the beginning of each school year. As classes visit the library throughout the year, the librarian reminds students when it's time to check out. Further steps include warning signs placed throughout the library and especially at the exits and the physical arrangement of the library itself to limit the number of exits. The principle is to let students know through multiple means that books shouldn't be taken unless checked out.

If this isn't enough, the next step is detection. This is where the alarm system comes into play, as is covered later in this chapter. It can also include physical detection of materials by librarians, staff, and teachers as students utilize the library and exit. With enough personnel, theft could conceivably be eliminated through these observations. However, the technology involved with a security system is a cost-saving device that's more efficient at schools that don't have the budget to hire enough people to watch everything that each student does in the library.

The final security stage is response. This involves catching students in the act of removing materials inappropriately and introducing library staff, other school personnel, or even security or police to deal with the situation. Such response is a deterrent to future stealing. If other students are aware of what happens it could even reinforce good behavior in the rest of the student body. Speak up and let the rest of the students hear when a student is caught. This isn't to say that every infraction requires a student to be embarrassed or intimidated into following the rules; it depends on the situation and the history of the student. Keep a record of student names to see if there is a trend in alarms.

One thing to consider is the intent of the student when materials are taken improperly. Is the student actually stealing or simply borrowing but forgetting procedure? Absentminded students aren't uncommon. Sometimes simply the presence of a security system is enough to jog their memories. Therefore, the ability to psychologically deter possible offenders might be the greatest strength of a security system.[2]

TYPES OF SECURITY SYSTEMS

There are a few basic types of security systems and then, of course, myriad vendor differences and add-on options. The systems can be divided into three main technologies: electromagnetic, radio frequency, and radio frequency identification.

Electromagnetic

Electromagnetic systems are the most prevalent in libraries today and are the middle ground for price and convenience. They work by placing a thin metallic strip three to seven inches long and made of a highly magnetic material inside the book with self-stick adhesive. Changing the status of the tags is accomplished magnetically. They are considered a "full circulation" system. The procedure is simple, adding a quick step to the check-in and checkout process. The librarian or staff turns off the security strip (deactivation) when students check out a book, and then turns it back on (reactivation) when it's checked back in. A book that's not deactivated will set off the alarm at the library exit when student attempts to walk out.

Varying terminology is used in regard to the activation and deactivation of security strips, also known as *tags*. You may hear the terms *deactivation*, *desensitizer*, or *demagnetizer* used interchangeably.

The metallic strips are fairly unobtrusive. They're easily placed within the spine of the book so that they don't interfere with the handling of the book, do the least amount of damage, and are invisible to students. The less that students know about the system the better. Don't let them see you processing the books or adding security strips. You want them to be unaware of the process so that they don't try to circumvent the system. Most school libraries don't have to worry about archival materials, but you do need to be aware that adhesives will degrade over time and damage paper. This almost negligible consequence in school libraries could come up in discussion.

Most school libraries aren't as concerned about magazines and journals simply because of the benefit-to-cost ratio. For some school libraries, new issues of journals arrive almost daily, which requires more tags and more processing time. You can place these strips between pages, as close to the binding as possible. To reduce the possibility of damage with photocopying and students trying to pull the pages apart to lay them flat, it's ideal to place the strip on pages of ads.

Electromagnetic systems are safe to use with electronic media. There are many benefits to having a system like this in place:

- Deters thieves by physical presence of electronic gates
- Protects your materials
- Provides reliable detection with minimal false alarms
- Complies with ADA (Americans with Disabilities Act) regulations as the exit pathway is open and clear

Radio Frequency

Radio frequency is a less-expensive option but is slightly less flexible and convenient. This type of system is often referred to as a pass around (by-pass) system. You can see bypass systems in place at certain stores, especially those with video/DVD/Blu-ray rentals, whereby your purchase is handed to you on the other side of the gate. The tags are always on. On the one hand, it saves time by not having to worry about activating and deactivating books at check-in and checkout, but on the other hand, it takes time to hand them around the gate. Depending on how the library is set up, this might be very impractical if not impossible. Nonetheless, when cost is an issue and if the layout of the library supports its use, the bypass system is a viable and often-used option.

One way of getting around this issue of the always-on tag is to simply block the tag by another means. By use of special date-due tabs or date-due cards to block the magnetized tag, the person at the checkout can eliminate having to bypass the gate. These magnetized tags are little squares that are placed on the inside back cover of a book. They aren't truly less obtrusive, but since they can be covered or hidden easily, they may attract less attention from a curious student. Many students wouldn't realize the purpose of the special due-date slips, but some may make the connection and use that knowledge either to circumvent the gates or for other reasons.

The benefits are similar to electromagnetic systems with one additional advantage. Since the technology uses radio waves instead of electromagnetic waves, you don't need to worry about the placement and distance of the exit gates in relation to computers and other electronic equipment. If space is an issue, you can easily have a computer just inches away from one of these gates without worry of damage.

Radio Frequency Identification

Radio frequency identification (RFID) has quickly sparked interest in many industries. Although Wal-Mart and other businesses are quickly moving into the possibilities, schools and libraries have been waiting for the prices to drop. A few libraries are early adopters, but it is still very rare to find RFID chips in library books. While widespread use of RFID chips is still a long way off, it does appear that in years to come RFID could take over as the predominant technology.

RFID chips continue to drop in price because of bulk purchases and their use throughout industry. This enhanced radio frequency allows for storage of information about each item as opposed to being a simple on or off device. Therefore, an RFID chip can combine the barcode and book identification with the security. Security gates can verify that books leaving the library are checked out.

Using radio waves simplifies the process of circulation and stack maintenance and even more so if barcode information is included on the RFID chip. With no physical laser or line of sight required, a scanner simply needs to be near the item to read the chip. Staff can inventory the shelves by slowly walking down the stacks, holding the scanner past each shelf. This could mean a reduction in time. Manual inventory sometimes takes weeks, inventories with barcodes may take a day or two, and inventories with RFID chips may only take minutes. Furthermore, checkout is also much faster. Instead of having to look for each barcode and manipulate the book to get it scanned, you can simply wave the book near the scanner in any direction. If you have a coordinated book drop system, you can have it automatically check in each book as it's placed in the book drop.

ADDITIONAL OPTIONS

A great deal of variation is based on the basic technology. Decisions could include the physical appearance of the exit gates in terms of design, color, height, size, and ease of installation. You can purchase add-on devices, such as locking swing arms that come down as alarms go off so that students are stopped from leaving. Turnstiles—which, incidentally, actually add ADA issues since they can make exiting difficult for some patrons—can slow exiting and add order to students leaving in groups so that students can be easily identified, being forced to walk through one by one. Security cameras, video surveillance systems, or closed circuit television, although rare in school libraries, can provide staff with a comfort of both physical safety and safety for the library materials.

Another option that's still expensive and rare in the school library—though it's gaining acceptance in academic and public libraries—is self-checkout systems. Over time, these will continue to drop in price. In combination with RFID, which eliminates the need for children to line up barcodes to lasers, the adoption of self-checkout systems in school libraries will only increase.[3]

DO I NEED A SECURITY SYSTEM?

The costs for security systems have been dropping over time and will continue to do so. A basic setup can cost as little as about $5,000. It's not unheard of to spend twice that, and if you start using RFID and self-checkout and other add-ons, the cost can continue to rise. You also need to keep in mind the cost for the tags. If you choose a common electromagnetic system, spine tags will only cost about 10¢ each. Although that might not sound like much, and in relation to the price of a book it may sound minimal, converting an entire library at one time can add up. Don't forget the additional and unforeseen costs, such as staff time for processing materials, which adds an extra step; installation, if this is a separate cost; service contracts; and time involved with false alarms.[4]

Because this is a large monetary investment and considerable time will be spent adding tags to books and materials, a thorough analysis should be performed. An inventory needs to be conducted each year, and the number of books and their prices need to be calculated. Don't forget to calculate in staff time, processing of materials, updating the catalog, shipping (if applicable), barcodes, and other expenses included besides simply the cost of the books and materials themselves. Some schools simply don't have that big of a theft issue. Some students forget to check out books but still return them, some mistakes are staff errors, and a good inventory will highlight some of these issues. Even with some loss, it's not worth it if the price of the security system is greater than the loss of books. Some schools might pay for the cost of the security system itself in a few years' time; others won't.

Examples of real-life instances can be eye opening. For instance, Kickapoo High School Library in Springfield, Missouri, lost 187 books (worth about $2,000) in 2001–2002. For some schools, that is a lot of money; for others, not very much. In this case, their materials budget was only $9,000 per year. How can a library keep up when proportionately they're losing such a large volume of materials? Why were they losing so many? Compare these numbers to Reed Middle School in the same district: they lost only 12 books (worth $200) in that same school year. This school had implemented a security system.[5]

On the other hand, the introduction of a detection system at the Bishop's Stortford High School in Hertfordshire, England, led to criticism of the library for being overly protective and "too security conscious."[6] So, local perceptions must be factored into these decisions. What are the costs? What is the benefit? Could other methods solve the problems? How will it impact library services?

Few elementary schools have security systems, while an increasing number of high schools do. It appears that there's a direct correlation between the grade level and the need for increased security. Although this is a broad generalization, school librarians need to thoroughly assess needs before making changes.

Of course, additional problems tend to creep up, as is often the case when you put kids and technology in the same room. Some of these problems aren't the fault of the students. It's possible that other items trigger your alarms, such as public library books or items from stores. There have been instances where certain metal objects have triggered the alarm: key rings, bicycle clips, braces, and even metal pins from surgery in student legs.[7] Sometimes students simply get mischievous. Jokers will pull off the tags and place them in friends' backpacks or simply place books in friends' bags to get them caught. Some students will experiment with aluminum foil or other materials in an attempt to shield the book from the gates. They might even try deactivating the tags with magnets or holding the books above or outside the range of the gates as they walk through. Observation by the librarian and staff is still important regardless of what tools you utilize.

Finally, as with many other things in the library, additional guidelines, policies, and procedures must be written, explained, and followed. Librarians and staff need to be consistent in terms of what they do when the alarm goes off. Furthermore, you don't want to create a negative environment by embarrassing honest students who make a mistake every once in a while. Additionally, if the mistake was a library worker's fault, own up to it. Speak loudly and let the other students hear that the student was doing nothing wrong. Use the security system to prevent theft, but don't let it get in the way of providing excellent service.

WEBSITES

3m: http://3m.com
Checkpoint Systems: www.checkpointsystems.com
DynaTag: www.dynataginc.com
Library Automation Technologies: www.latcorp.com
Sentry Technology: www.sentrytechnology.com

NOTES

1. Lawrence J. Fennelly, *Handbook of Loss Prevention and Crime Prevention* (Boston: Butterworth-Heinemann, 1996), 395.

2. Bradley Tolppanen, "Electronic Detection Systems: Is Your Library Ready for One?" *Louisiana Libraries* 63, no. 2 (Fall 2000): ¶4.

3. Walter Minkel, "Gotcha!" *School Library Journal* 48, no. 10 (October 2002): 55.

4. Betty J. Morris, *Administering the School Library Media Center* (Westport, CT: Libraries Unlimited, 2004), 517.

5. Minkel, "Gotcha!" 5.

6. Tolppanen, "Electronic Detection Systems," ¶20.

7. Helen Knox, "How Are We Doing? A Security System in a School Library," *The School Librarian* 42 (November 1994): 142.

12

Technology Plans

> Acting as a technologist (rather than a technician) and a collaborator with teachers, the library media specialist plays a critical role in designing student experiences that focus on authentic learning, information literacy, and curricular mastery—not simply on manipulating machinery.[1]

This is a key difference between school librarians and library staff, and between school librarians and technical staff. School librarians understand how technology, and in turn information access and literacy, is incorporated into learning. Technical staff knows how to set up computers and equipment, but they might not know the specific needs of teachers and students. School librarians see the big picture through each and every grade level, classroom, teacher, and student. Planning is required in order to successfully move the library and the school into the future. Though the future is a moving target and is constantly in motion, thoughtful planning can make the best use of finances and resources.

Technology plans have been around since the early days of libraries, schools, and technology. Initially, they were informal and simply a by-product of good leadership and forward thinking. As with anything in the library or in life, it's ideal to plan ahead. By not doing so, you leave yourself open to a piecemeal and unstructured approach that creates a haphazard development process. Time and money are spent on things that might not be needed or that don't mesh well with what you already have. The process can be seen in light of how we might decorate a home. Ideally, you have a picture in your mind about how it's styled, how the pieces of furniture fit, the colors of the walls, the lighting, the organization, and so on. Without planning, nothing will match, you and your spouse may separately buy two sofas when you only need one, and you might miss opportunities when sales arise because you are unprepared. When working with limited budgets, be sure to move the library in the direction you need, that everything works together, and that you acquire what's most beneficial to student learning. You don't want to invest heavily in the latest fad only to find out the next year that it's not being used.

Proper planning is a given for anyone in a leadership or management role. Even an informal back-of-an-envelope process is better than nothing. However, developments have pushed school libraries into creating formalized plans for their own good. The first formal and required technology plans were developed as grant proposals for Title III of the Elementary and Secondary Education Act during late 1970s.[2] Today, because of the Library Services and Technology Act and to obtain E-rate assistance, schools and their libraries continue to write their technology plans in coordination with long-range planning. This financial impetus is a strong motivator. Regardless of the reason, it's still a good idea to have a technology plan. It just so happens that there are now requirements to do so.

A school library technology plan can be seen a roadmap. Proper planning is needed so that you don't get lost and so that you can see the direction you should be moving the library in. Working heavily with new technologies that change monthly, there's a constant need to stay current on trends and advances. There'll always be a need for upgrades, additions, replacements, and even moving toward services that were unheard of just a few years back. Hardware, software, and multiple devices need to be planned for or you'll continually be unprepared. However, the emphasis of preparing a technology plan isn't on the end result but rather on the process itself. The key to writing a good technology plan is communication.

WHAT IS A TECHNOLOGY PLAN?

A technology plan is a document that states the long-term aims and objectives for the use of information technology in the school or school library media center and indicates in broad terms how these will be achieved. This plan could take three possible routes.[3]

First and most commonly, the school library is simply included in the larger parent organization plan, whether that's at the district and/or school level. While the library is certainly covered in this scenario and the librarian should be involved as a member of this team and as part of the process, the library is simply seen as part of the overall larger picture.

Second, the library's technology plan is incorporated within the library's overall strategic or long-range plan. In this case, although there's still a district or school technology plan, the library technology plan is an incorporated piece of the library long-range plan that includes many other components.

Third, the library has a stand-alone technology plan that's completely independent and separate from the school/district. This could occur when the librarian is not involved on the school/district committee. The reason for doing a separate plan is to make it easier for your own budgeting process and for grant writing. It can be difficult to sort out the library from the school in a large plan—especially in the case of a large district. Smaller schools are much easier to combine everything in one. Therefore, you might decide to create both a library plan that can be incorporated into the larger school or district plan. Both plans could be modified later so that they mesh, but it would be helpful to have both for different needs.

Regardless of the approach taken, the librarian needs to be aware of what's needed in the library. You can't haphazardly buy technology for the library and hope that it'll all work together. You need to know what's needed before grants come along and before money is found. Otherwise you'll be scrambling at the last minute and most likely not making the best decisions.

It's also very important to include professional development, training, and teaching within the technology plan. The plan itself is more than a simple list of hardware and software to buy. To be most effective, it must include the components to make the purchases effective and purposeful. A district technology plan should focus on integrating technology into the teaching and learning process to transform the way teachers teach and students learn. At the very least, the technology plan should be embedded in or supplement the district's comprehensive school improvement plan.

Furthermore, the process can't stand alone in terms of student learning. All proposals should be tied to curriculum and state standards, district and state goals. To do this effectively and to tie everything together, the technology plan can't be done by a single person. It should involve a large committee of people with vested interests: administrators, teachers, technology support staff, students, parents, and the community.

When the plan is written, it must be understood that it's always in motion. While this planning is important to guide the direction of technology in the library and the school, it's unrealistic to look ahead much further than five years because of the constant change of what's available. Furthermore, even over that five-year time span, the plan will need to be continually updated and revised as needed. The technology plan is a process that helps us look to the future, but it's not set in stone. The process of writing it allows us to spend the time to think and reflect on our needs. We need to be continually thinking about technology issues, so the plan never is really finished but is instead a work in progress and a guide to help us think.

THE PROCESS OF CREATING THE PLAN

The process of preparing to write the technology plan, regardless of the size or organizational structure of the school, is the following:

- Preplanning
- Data collection of current technology
- Establishment of goals
- Production of action plan
- Dissemination, monitoring, and evaluation

Although the finer details can be tweaked from school to school, these broad categories ensure that the process is orderly and complete. If you look closely at the order, you'll notice that it follows the outline of a simple instructional design model that's cyclical in nature. By completing the cycle with evaluation, it leads back to the beginning to reevaluate the plan in a continual process of updating and refocusing the needs and goals.

Preplanning

The most important step in preparing a technology plan is getting a good committee together. Involve all of the stakeholders. The number of people on the committee will vary from school to school as smaller or larger schools will naturally have more or less complexity to work with. A large-city school district is a much larger endeavor than a single rural school. Regardless, these types of people can be involved on a technology planning committee:

- One superintendent or other central office administrator
- One principal
- Two technology coordinators, computer teachers, or other technology professionals
- One library media specialist
- Three teachers, representing different buildings, grades, and/or content areas
- Two students
- One board member and/or school committee member
- One support staff
- Three parents
- One community or town official
- One higher-education representative
- One business expert/representative

This might seem like a lot of people, but everyone involved plays a different role and has a different perspective. It's possible for committees to become unwieldy if they become too large and ineffective if they're too small. However, when it comes to technology, there's a need for such collaboration and input. There are many different sections of the technology plan to write, so the work can be divided.

With a technology planning committee in place, there are some key first steps. First, if there's a current technology plan, it should be read and reviewed by everyone on the committee to understand what's been done in the past. Second, as with all committees, a structure should be determined for meeting dates and times and a timeline established for completion of the new technology plan.

At this point, the committee will set the framework for the rest of the plan by writing or reviewing and updating the basic premise of technology in that school. This involves a vision statement and a technology mission statement. Schools and libraries should already have vision and mission statements. They probably already include a statement or section on technology. These separate and distinct statements on technology allow the formation of a more specific definition that sets the stage for the committee's work. Without the technology vision and mission, it would be difficult for the technology plan committee to truly understand the direction in which they should head.

Data Collection of Current Technology

Once the preplanning has been completed, the next step is to gather information. To plan for the future, you need to know what you have right now. Thus, a complete inventory of current technology must be created. Much of this data should already be collected on a continual basis. A well-run organization keeps an updated inventory as technology comes in, goes out, and is moved. However, some of this information might be in different places, and different people might be responsible for different areas. Therefore, the task becomes one of piecing together all of the different sources, as well as double-checking to ensure that the information is accurate.

To truly understand the current state of technology, one needs to go beyond simply listing an inventory. While this is an important first step, the next step is to comprehend how each piece of technology is used and what's lacking. Therefore, this data collection should include surveying and observing so that you can see the present level of use.[4] Furthermore, an indication of the estimated life cycle of the item and the remaining life left will help to provide information for decision making. For example, it is much more informative if all of the computers are at the end of their life cycle than simply indicating the number of computers currently in place.

Establishment of Goals

The next step is to use the information that's been gathered in conjunction with the vision and mission technology statements to establish goals for the next few years. This requires a fair amount of research into current trends in technology use, discussions on how best to integrate technology into the curriculum, a commitment to professional development so that teachers and other professionals understand how to use the technology that's purchased, and, especially, discussions on how funding will be accomplished to meet these goals.

The goals should include both broad generalizations and specifics. It's nice to dream of what you could do with an unlimited budget, but it's best to focus on what's realistic and achievable. This doesn't mean to sell yourself short and ask for too little. On the other hand, don't ask for too much. Ask for what you think you can expect, but be prepared to acquire additional technologies if you find additional money somewhere. This type of document should focus on what you can do and how you will accomplish it. It should still be adaptable so it can be modified in terms of timeline and actions, but the goal is to set forth a plan that you'll be able to accomplish.

After the goals are developed, you'll need to form objectives for each goal. Measurements of the accomplishments that support the goals, objectives are

- clear,
- concise and to the point,
- measurable,
- adaptable to timelines and action plans, and
- observable.

Production of Action Plan

With goals and objectives in place, the next step is to produce an action plan. The plan should describe each step, define a timeline, and list the person or persons responsible. A heading might look like table 12.1. Below each action step, be specific as to what action will occur. Make it very clear as to what will take place, what will be purchased, and how it will be completed. Be specific as to when the action will be completed by and who'll be completing this action. When completed, it should be very easy to check

Table 12.1. Sample Action Plan Heading

Action Step	Timeline	Person Responsible

Table 12.2.　Sample Action Step

Action Step	Timeline	Person Responsible
Upgrade RAM in five library computers from 512 MB to 1.5 GB	By the end of the first year	Librarian

off completed action steps and thus to know exactly where you stand in accomplishing your goals. An example of a simple action step is shown in table 12.2.

To be entirely effective, your plan must address professional development for faculty/staff training as well as specific action steps integrating technology into the learning process. A plan concentrating only on hardware and software purchases lacks overall effectiveness. The key to all of these steps is technology involved in the learning process. Little will be accomplished if things are the key issue and not students. Action plans, when completed, should allow teachers to teach more effectively and create positive results throughout the school.

Dissemination, Monitoring, and Evaluation

With an action plan in hand, the next step is carry out that plan, make purchases, and put the new technology in place and into use. An important part of this process is clear oversight to be sure that those responsible are completing their tasks. It's very easy at this step to assume someone else is taking care of everything. With the busy workplaces we have, these purchases, if moved out of sight, can completely disappear from our radar screen and be forgotten until the end of the year, or worse. It can be truly disappointing to find out that money has been lost because items weren't ordered or followed up on.

It's also important that they and others publicize the progress being made and the changes taking place. While professional development is always part of this, many steps are invisible to the school at large. Therefore, it's a good idea to keep everyone informed about the goings-on throughout the school. A variety of different methods can be used to inform the school and stakeholders in the progress being made. This could include, among other avenues the following:

- School and district newsletters
- Technology demonstrations at school committee meetings
- School open houses
- School Web pages and/or e-mail

The school or districts technology committee should continually monitor the implementation process to ensure that it's on track. Goals and objectives can be continually reviewed, and tasks can be modified as pricing
changes or additional tools or components are unexpectedly found to be
required. Teachers, students, and those using the new technologies should
be evaluated in multiple ways to ensure that the actions are meeting the
goals set and that student learning is improved.

WRITING THE PLAN: BASIC COMPONENTS

Now that we have talked about the process of writing the plan, we can move
on to the actual document itself—how it's organized and what to include.
Although technology plans vary considerably, as well they should because
of their individualized nature, the basic components are

- Executive summary
- Background information
- Current state of technology
- Technology plan and budget
- Evaluation

Some of these sections might sound familiar after going through the plan
process earlier. The process itself is used to write the plan, and sections will
therefore mirror each other to some extent. However, a formal document
will still require an organization and structure that won't be written linearly.
We will look at each section a little closer.

Executive Summary

A formal document like a library, school, or district technology plan requires an executive summary at the very front. This provides the reader with
a brief and succinct overview of what the document is and what to expect.
Depending on the complexity and size of the plan, this could require as
little as a paragraph or two or at most a page. The key is brevity and sum-
marization.

Background Information

The next section provides background information to describe the foundation for the upcoming recommendations. The more thorough you can
be, the more precise and accurate of a plan will be produced.

This section includes an overview of the library and/or the school/ district, mission statements, detailed information about the users and the community, a description of the process and who was involved, the context of the plan, including the underlying values, assumptions that were considered during plan preparation, references to related and/or previous plans, and anything else that you might want to include.

Some plans will take it a step further and include a SWOT analysis. SWOT stands for

- Strengths
- Weaknesses
- Opportunities
- Threats

A SWOT analysis is usually viewed as a matrix (see table 12.3).

Strengths and weaknesses can be viewed as existing internal resources or capabilities. Alternately, opportunities and threats are external factors that could affect the school's options. By describing the environment, technology, and related factors that have an impact on technology choices, a good overview of the situation can be identified as a basis for decision making.

Current State of Technology

The section on the current state of technology is the inventory that was previously mentioned. To determine where you want to go in the future, you need to first understand where you are, what's working, and what's not. This is often overlooked because people tend to think that they already know what they have. However, we must not forget that a lot of people on the committee might not have the big picture as to all the different technologies that exist. Furthermore, this detailed description will be the evidence needed to demonstrate support for requested new tools and technologies.

Technology Plan and Budget

The bulk of the plan and the part that everything leads up to is the actual technology plan with the corresponding budget. This will consist of specific goals, objectives, activities, and initiatives. It'll include timelines, responsible parties, specific technologies to purchase, and their prices.

Table 12.3.   SWOT Matrix

Strengths	Weaknesses
Opportunities	Threats

Although it's difficult to generalize, technology plan committees should remember to look at the entire picture and all of the additional costs involved. For instance, for every dollar spent on technology, a general rule is that 40 percent will go toward hardware, 20 percent for software, another 20 percent for professional development, and an additional 20 percent for upgrades and unexpected future needs.[5]

Evaluation

As touched on in the previous section on preparing the plan, the continuous and ongoing evaluation of technology used throughout the curriculum is an important step in the process. Through the use of data collection rubrics, student artifacts, surveys, tests, and other evaluation materials, teachers and administrators can ensure that effective learning is taking place.[6]

The evaluation section is also important to ensure that the plan is being carried out successfully, that technology is being purchased and used as requested, and that faculty training and development is taking place. Timelines and benchmarks need to be reviewed as this is the committee with the oversight to ensure that they are taking place.

THE DIFFERENCE BETWEEN A GOOD
AND A BAD TECHNOLOGY PLAN

So what makes a technology plan at one school better than a plan at another? Beyond the basics of the included components and ensuring that the plan is complete, consider the following while writing your plan.

A good plan is

- concise;
- specific—not only explains what, but why;
- library-user centered—needs assessment is important;
- related to library mission and parent organization;
- logical—obvious, coherent progression and structure;
- readable;
- flexible—modular in structure for ease of updating;
- complete—provides all the information the reader needs.

A bad plan

- doesn't explain why;
- doesn't relate to mission;
- doesn't relate to needs of users;

- doesn't have a logical structure;
- doesn't present all the information a reader needs;
- is poorly formatted.

WEBSITES

Technology Planning (DESE): http://dese.mo.gov/divimprove/instrtech/techplan/gettingstarted.htm
Educational Technology Fact Sheet: www.ed.gov/about/offices/list/os/technology/facts.html
National Education Technology Plan: www.nationaledtechplan.org
NCLB: www.ed.gov/nclb/landing.jhtml
NETS Standards: www.iste.org/AM/Template.cfm?Section=NETS

NOTES

1. American Association of School Librarians and Association for Educational Communications and Technology, *Information Power: Building Partnerships for Learning* (Chicago: American Library Association, 1998), 54.

2. John M. Cohn, Ann L. Kelsey, and Keith Michael Fiels, *Writing and Updating Technology Plans* (New York: Neal-Schuman, 1999), 16.

3. Joseph R. Matthews, *Technology Planning: Preparing and Updating a Library Technology Plan* (Westport, CT: Libraries Unlimited, 2004), 2.

4. Harvey Bennett, "Successful K–12 Technology Planning: Ten Essential Elements," *Teacher Librarian* 31, no. 1 (October 2003): 22.

5. Bennett, "Successful K–12 Technology Planning," 24.

6. Bennett, "Successful K–12 Technology Planning," 24.

5

TECHNOLOGY AND THE TEACHING COMPONENT

13

Professional Development

·

In this final part of the book, we look closer at the teaching component of technology use from the school librarian's perspective. Although we can't cover everything in regard to teaching with or about technology and although some of this has already been touched upon, the focus here is on professional development and lifelong learning. We must stay abreast of technology changes and the production and dissemination of handouts and printed materials. Keeping knowledge and information to ourselves isn't productive and doesn't serve our students well. Use professional development as an opportunity to make the library even more visible.

Educators, of all people, understand the need for lifelong learning. Continuing education in multiple forms ensures that we keep up with changes in information literacy, with technology in the school library, and with other aspects of libraries and schools. Technology has been tightly linked to information literacy, and a great deal of effort must be spent keeping up with changes in our profession. The library of today looks far different than from 20 years ago, and it'll surely look quite different in another 20 years. This implies that those who are working in the school and the library must keep up with those changes through ongoing professional development.

Professional development is important for ourselves as well as those we work with. This chapter focuses on our involvement with helping others develop their skills and knowledge. Librarians have a great deal to share with teachers and administrators. Without sharing changes in the library and those concerning how to access and utilize resources, our library patrons won't be able to adequately find the information they need. This in turn will lessen the importance of the library in their eyes.

Librarians already teach students about the library and what services and resources are provided. Special attention must be given to teachers as well. We have more to share than many first realize. We might also be involved with determining the needs of school staff, arranging development with other teachers, and providing support. The school librarian is in a key position to offer as well as lead professional development throughout the school.

Information Power clearly defines one of the major responsibilities of the school librarian as filling the role of "instructional consultant." The most basic level of consultation is simply introducing teachers to what the library has to offer.[1] Principle 9 stresses the need to have a well-publicized library program.[2] Awareness of new services, resources, and tools is the first step.

Principle 8 takes this awareness idea further and talks about the need for ongoing staff development for librarians, both to maintain professional knowledge and skills and to provide instruction in information literacy for teachers, administrators, and other members of the learning community.[3] Ongoing staff development is considered an essential component of the library media program.

The goals listed in these principles include maintaining current knowledge of the research and best practices of the field, working to obtain a budget for opportunities, collaborating to determine the school's needs, and fulfilling the requirement to "offer and promote an ongoing staff development program for the full school community, particularly in the integration of information technology and the use of the information literacy standards for student learning."[4]

We can teach the teachers about what the library has to offer. We can also teach about technologies around the school. Beyond doing the teaching ourselves, we can either find outside professional development opportunities for teachers and staff, or we can coordinate the sharing of skills and information among everyone already in the school. Some schools have found this to be quite effective. By utilizing their own staff, equipment, and facilities, these in-house experts can easily and inexpensively teach each other. Those involved with the teaching can run the entire range of the school, including teachers, technology support staff, and principals, and some schools have even included the superintendent.[5]

Many schools have administrators who recognize the valuable role the school librarian can have. In many instances, the principal realizes the importance of working with the librarian to determine what staff development programs are needed. Development must, however, be planned and purposeful. Time and money spent on programs that faculty and staff consider a waste of time won't boost morale and will only make future development endeavors more difficult to accept.

Determining what educators need or want to learn about can be done in several ways. The most straightforward is simply to ask teachers what they want to learn. However, sometimes people don't know what to ask. It can be difficult to clearly ask for that which you don't know. Therefore, a detailed survey with possible suggestions is an ideal option or alternative. These surveys could be linked to new software or hardware that the school has obtained or ideas, trends, and techniques that are uncovered at conferences, during reading the literature, or visiting other schools and participating in professional organizations. This could also include observing teachers and seeing how they interact or don't interact with technology in their lessons, using assessment rubrics, or reviewing student standardized test scores. This place is ideal for librarians to collaborate with teachers for increasing technology use in the classroom. While open-ended requests and suggestions for development should always be considered, a more structured approach is often likely to be very effective. The most structured approach would be to work with companies such as iAssessment or Co-nect Tech, which provide detailed evaluations of teacher skills based on National Education Technology standards. Professional development should be fair, consistent, progressive, and meaningful.[6]

PROBLEMS TO OVERCOME

All schools have some type of professional development plan in place and often a committee and/or a person overseeing professional development for the school. The question is how involved the school librarian is with these plans. Time and energy is always part of the problem when people want to participate; resistance in the form of lack of participation and cost issues need to be overcome.

By utilizing our own experts in our own schools and districts, some of the professional development cost is reduced. There are still some costs involved with paying for substitutes if this development is conducted during a normal school day. Sometimes this can be scheduled for days when children aren't in class.

Time involvement is a big issue. Teachers are already overwhelmed and if the only time you plan professional development is after school, attendance and participation will be much lower. Ideally, the administration will provide support in this area and will accommodate schedules and time for teachers to meet during the school day.

Some teachers are naturally reluctant to change their teaching styles. They might feel that professional development means that what they've done in the past or what they're currently doing isn't good enough if they're expected to learn new ideas and technologies. There's also a fear of making mistakes with technology, breaking it, or simply not knowing how to use it effectively. There are many ways to work with these reluctant teachers.[7]

First, remember that enthusiasm is contagious. Work with those teachers who are truly interested in learning and trying new things. Once others see their success and hear about what they've done, others might want to join in.

Next, talk with people outside of your school who work with technology integration. This may include those in a regional or statewide organization, in other districts, or at conferences. Learn how others have faced similar circumstances.

Publicize your success. Let everyone know about the positive changes that have taken place. If the development occurs in a vacuum, then how will others benefit from those successes?

Technology is constantly changing, but keep in mind that this can also include nontechnology-related topics. Any way that the librarian can be involved with improving the school, the curriculum, or other aspects of education will only benefit the library in the future.

EXAMPLES OF PROFESSIONAL DEVELOPMENT TECHNOLOGY TOPICS

The many standard types of professional development sessions can range from basic informational presentations, to introductory lessons, to more advanced seminars. These sessions can include technology directly or in a cursory manner. Some possible topics include the following:

- Digital cameras
- PDAs (personal digital assistants)
- Specific devices, such as Averkey, Intellitools, or Alphasmart
- Electronic white boards
- OPAC (online public access catalog)
- Databases
- Website video subscriptions, such as United Streaming or Brainpop
- WebQuests or iAdventures
- Plagiarism and copyright information and resources
- Ergonomics
- Network basics, firewalls
- Filters
- Accelerated Reader/Scholastic Reading Counts

- Software, such as Photoshop, Inspiration, Microsoft Office, or OpenOffice
- Web 2.0 resources

Teachers might be interested in a multitude of different software programs, so it largely depends on what the school has purchased. New software is continually being developed, and new versions are constantly being offered. Remember that your teachers probably run the entire line from novice to advanced. Some teachers still need help with the very basics of Microsoft Word, e-mail, and how to add attachments. Never assume that all of the teachers are at the same level. There'll always be a need to help those who are slightly (or more) behind the curve.

There are several different ways to reach teachers. The most effective in terms of reaching the greatest number of people at a single time is simply the traditional large-group session. However, don't let that stop you from working with smaller groups or even one-on-one. Subsets of teachers might have a specific need, in which case the entire school doesn't need to be involved. Furthermore, informal instruction, which can be offered on the fly, is often overlooked but should be included in your record keeping. Many of these informal situations are important because they can make you aware of future session topics that others may be interested in. Finally, don't be afraid to take advantage of the opportunity to teach the teacher at the same time you're instructing students. It's entirely possible that a teacher might not have had the chance to learn about that particular topic. By teaching everyone together and being honest about it instead of embarrassed, it becomes an opportunity not only for the teacher to learn but also for the students to see that lifelong learning continues, even for teachers.

Remember to relax and keep in mind that while teaching peers/teachers is different than teaching children, we are in this together. Define your audience and modify your lesson for your particular needs, whether that is teaching a group of teachers, administrators, staff, paraprofessionals, or a combination thereof. Teach them not only how to use these technologies, but also how to use them in the classroom with specific lessons in mind.

DESIGNING A SUCCESSFUL IN-SERVICE

The steps involved with offering a successful professional development session might sound familiar to you because they're based on common instructional methods we're all familiar with. It's easy, however, to forget about these concepts as the setting isn't your traditional library or classroom. So, too, your students aren't the children that you're involved with every day but instead your peers and coworkers. Therefore, when you have the opportunity to provide an instructional session, remember the following.

First, assess yourself and the audience. Perform a needs assessment to determine precisely what the audience needs. Get input from the teachers so that you're providing something worthwhile. There's nothing more frustrating than to sit through a lesson that isn't what you had expected and that you don't want to learn about.

Second, analyze the learner. Adults are special learners. Know their level of expertise. Be sure to have administrative support.

Third, select your instructional objectives. Specify what the teachers should know at the end of the session.

Fourth, provide incentives for those attending if you can. Extrinsic motivation is sometimes required to overcome teachers' initial reluctance. Work with your administrators to see what can be done in this area. This could include release time, credit, recognition, and certificates. At a minimum, try to provide snacks or little prizes.

Fifth, plan materials and activities that relate to the audience and objectives. Make it practical. Conduct small sessions to break it up, as opposed to a single long day that can be overwhelming. Provide worksheets, include an agenda, produce a tip sheet as a handout, and utilize a teacher as an assistant if possible. Most of all, be flexible and keep it simple. It also doesn't hurt to have a good sense of humor.

Sixth, utilize guided practice. Allowing the participants to use the new knowledge while you're present reinforces the learning and provides an opportunity to diagnose the need for further instruction.

Seventh, try to involve small groups rather than large ones. Avoid required attendance unless you can't avoid it. Forced attendance is difficult to motivate.

Eighth, evaluate the in-service. Circulating a simple feedback form and making a brief list of things to add, change, or delete the next time can add to the effectiveness of future workshops.

And finally, ninth, continue to be available to teachers after the in-service.

WEBSITES

Accelerated Reader: www.renlearn.com/ar/
BrainPOP: www.brainpop.com
iAssessment: www.iassessment.com
IntelliTools: www.intellitools.com
NEO: www.neo-direct.com/intro.aspx

Smart Technologies: www.smarttech.com
United Streaming: www.unitedstreaming.com

NOTES

1. American Association of School Librarians and Association for Educational Communications and Technology, *Information Power: Building Partnerships for Learning* (Chicago: American Library Association, 1998), 113.

2. American Association of School Librarians, *Information Power: Building Partnerships*, 112.

3. American Association of School Librarians, *Information Power: Building Partnerships*, 111.

4. American Association of School Librarians, *Information Power: Building Partnerships*, 112.

5. Mary A. Anderson, "Creating Tech-Savvy Teachers," *School Library Journal* 49, no. 2 (February 2003): 6.

6. Scott M. Hannon, "Building a Better Staff," *School Library Journal* 49, no. 2 (February 2003): 4.

7. Wesley A. Fryer, "Working with Reluctant Teachers," *Technology & Learning* 25, no. 11 (June 2005): 12.

14

Instructional Handouts and Materials

There are multiple ways of conveying instruction or reinforcing what's been taught through printed materials. In a school library setting, much of what's taught is presented orally, with direct interaction between students and teachers/librarians. Of course, technology can be used in many ways as part of this process. As mentioned, there are many opportunities to create instructional materials that can be easily shared electronically, such as via websites, WebQuests, or iAdventures. These are easy to update; given ample computers, easy to use as part of the lesson or for guidance after the lesson; and save paper and other associated printing costs.

However, sometimes you simply need to have something in print. Print materials are easy to take outside of the library or classroom, are easily accessible, and are easier to follow when trying to do something on the computer screen in another program. Not long ago, paper was the only option. With new technology, the production of these print materials is easier than ever.

Instructional handouts and materials can be used in a variety of ways. They often accompany a presentation by the librarian or can be used by students as a way to remember the lesson. They can even be used as stand-alone instruction where students can learn a quick procedure on their own. Furthermore, they can be useful for any library visitor, whether student or teacher. They can always be handed out when needed or even stored in some type of display, taped on a wall, or included as instructions with checkout for electronic devices for immediate readiness.

The earliest form of printed instructional material is the pathfinder, which has been relegated to lesser use and is often converted into equivalent electronic formats. The pathfinder is a document that guides a student to the resources the library has on a specific topic. The librarian creates and updates these ahead of time by knowing what topics teachers are using in their lessons. This saves time for the librarian because he or she doesn't have to answer the same questions asked repeatedly by each and every student. The pathfinder lists some of the books owned by the library on that topic, with call numbers, and sometimes separates the titles into fiction, nonfiction, reference, and other categories. The list might include journals and even relevant article titles. There might also be materials in other formats, such as DVDs, sound recordings, and even websites.

The pathfinder is a guiding hand that makes the process of finding appropriate materials easy for the student. Some might argue that the student doesn't learn about the organization of the library and how to find materials on their own with this kind of support. However, because the preparation of pathfinders can't be done for every topic because of time constraints, there's still ample time for students to work on those other skills.

In the early days, handouts were created with typewriters, carbon paper, and mimeograph machines. We've come a long way. Schools that don't have a large budget can still do a fine job because the most common tools are so far beyond what was once available. With a simple copy of Microsoft Office (Word and PowerPoint specifically), Open Office, or other word processors and presentation tools, you can do just about anything you need. But if you really want to go that extra mile, you can use more advanced and complex programs, such as Microsoft Publisher. A step up from that is Adobe PageMaker, which is considered the standard for small businesses. Beyond that are programs that would be overkill for a school library, yet you might have heard about: QuarkXPress or Adobe InDesign. Cost is usually the deciding factor as limited budgets often make it difficult to justify anything too expensive.

Clip art and image collections can add to what you create. A digital camera and a flatbed scanner can also increase the amount of personalized images to really drive home the instruction. Additional software, such as PhotoShop, Gimp, or SnagIt, can also make for much more graphic-rich and easier-to-follow directions.

Most people use the common word processor or a more complex publishing program. However, often-overlooked presentation tools, such as Microsoft PowerPoint, can be used with surprisingly easy and creative results.[1] The trick is to change the size of the slide to 8½″ x 11″ (or whatever paper size you are using) under File | Page Setup or the Design tab and then Page Setup in more recent versions. Using a blank presentation style, you are then free to add text, insert clip art, create autoshapes, draw lines and boxes and other shapes, insert images, and more.

On a side note, you aren't limited to a standard 8½" x 11" sheet of paper. You can continue enlarging the size of the slide to print on legal size paper and much larger. PowerPoint has set limits of up to 56 inches wide and high. This would allow you to create poster-size prints. Because the size of the monitor screen is much smaller, it does take some adjustment to zoom in and out and move left and right and up and down in order to work on such a large slide, but it does work. The only problem is that most schools won't have a printer that can handle poster-size paper. Therefore, you would need to take the file to a local copy center for printing.

PowerPoint also has the ability to group and ungroup sections. This makes working with objects much easier. If you have many different shapes and text boxes, having to add and move one can have an impact on many others. By grouping objects, you can move several items as one.

Finally, PowerPoint even includes a simple crop tool so that you can edit images directly. You therefore don't need to bother with external software for cropping images that you might want to use to explain certain steps in your handouts. To use the crop feature, choose the Crop icon from the floating Picture toolbar.

POSSIBLE INSTRUCTIONAL MATERIALS TOPICS

Countless topics can be covered in printed handouts and instructional materials. Some are generic in the sense that they could be used from one library to the next. Others could be specific to devices and models of items the library has purchased. Materials can include directions in a stepwise fashion or an overview of background information on a concept. Some examples include the following:

- Using the digital camera
- Using the online catalog
- Evaluating Web sources
- Using specific programs (PowerPoint, etc.)
- Citing references
- Using databases
- Searching the Internet (search engines, etc.)
- Using the Dewey Decimal System
- Using Accelerated Reader
- Using print resources (almanacs, encyclopedias, etc.)
- Honoring copyright
- Identifying and avoiding plagiarism
- Following the conduct code and acceptable technology use

DESIGN TIPS

Design techniques are important to consider. Although the content of what you're sharing with students and others is important, if it isn't clearly explained then that information is lost in the translation. Keep the following in mind.

KISS

KISS is an acronym for "Keep It Simple, Stupid." Basically, this means that you want to cut the instruction down to the bare minimum. You only have one or two pages, so there's no room for extraneous details. Furthermore, by getting to the point is easier for students to follow. Students shouldn't have to wade through the page trying to figure out what to do next.

Clear Directions

Not only should the directions be simple, but they should be clear. Think about the reading level of your students and the terminology they understand. Define and explain words and/or show images when necessary.

Short Sentences

Use short sentences or sentence fragments when you can. In fact, bullet points are much easier to follow. Students don't need to read an essay and have a hard time separating all of the steps when overwhelmed with text. Keep the text to a minimum.

Screen Capture

A picture is worth a thousand words. It can be very difficult to explain in words something that the student should see on a screen. Use a screen capture and edit it as necessary. You might want to crop the image or add highlights, shapes, arrows, lines, or text to clarify what they're seeing. This might take up precious space on a handout, but it can be much more enlightening than trying to describe using words.

Images and Clip Art

Images that support the directions other than screen captures are often great ideas. If you're trying to explain the parts of a digital camera, then take a picture of the camera and point out what and where the components are.

Clip art and image collections can be readily purchased to make the handout clearer and to add some liveliness to make it more attractive. Of course, nothing beats taking your own pictures to personalize the handout with just about anything you can think of.

Fonts and Colors

Various fonts and colors can be used to make the handout attractive to students. A boring page is more likely overlooked. Remember the age level of your students and what keeps them interested. On the other hand, don't overdo it. Multiple fonts and conflicting colors can detract from the content.

One Piece of Paper

At times, longer handouts are needed, but try to keep them to only one or two pages. Thus, only a single sheet of double-sided printing is required. Students are more apt to follow something that they can easily visualize from start to finish. Even if something longer is needed, see if you can break it down into chunks so that a single sheet covers a specific part of the process.

Balance, Proportion, Focus, and Unity

No matter how you lay out the pages, most good designs follow some basic principles.[2] Whether symmetrical or asymmetrical, the page should be balanced between text, images, and white space. The handout should not appear haphazard. Each of the elements should also be proportionate in relation to each other part. Nothing should stand out so much that it seems out of place with the rest of the page. In regard to focus, you should think about how the page is arranged so that the student can easily follow along and important pieces of information stand out. Finally, the page should be united into a coherent whole. The individual steps and pieces come together to create a single handout and it should appear as one.

Advertise

Put your name on the handout to ensure that you get credit. Furthermore, put the name of the school and library on it. Use this as a publicity tool so that every time someone looks at it, they will think about all the great things the library has to offer. Don't be shy about getting credit.

LEGAL CONCERNS

Librarians, of all people, know better than to take someone else's work and redistribute it. However, it might be tempting to copy and share the handouts and other instructional materials from a professional conference with everyone at your school. Consider many points before doing so.[3] Unless there's a statement on the material that specifically states that it can be copied for educational nonprofit purposes, then assume it isn't in the public domain and instead is under copyright protection. Simply ask the presenter at the end of the workshop. If you don't get the chance at the conference, then e-mail or snail mail the presenter afterward. Getting a print or electronic response is also good for permanent record keeping. If they say no, don't copy or redistribute their material. Under Fair Use, you could use a portion of it, talk about it, or even show it via a document camera, but that's it.

WEBSITES

The Ten Commandments of Computer Ethics: www.cpsr.org/issues/ethics/cei

NOTES

1. D. S. Brandt, "Create Your Own 'Quick-and-Dirty' Handouts," *Computers in Libraries* 22, no. 2 (February 2002): 39.

2. John Maxymuk, *Using Desktop Publishing to Create Newsletters, Handouts, and Web Pages: A How-to Do It Manual* (New York, Neal-Schuman, 1997), 31.

3. Rebecca P. Butler, "Workshop Handouts—Can I Share Them with My Colleagues?" *Knowledge Quest* 33, no. 2 (November/December 2004): 71.

15

Web 2.0

Many aspects of Web 2.0 have been touched upon throughout the chapters of this book, but it seems appropriate to tie them together and provide a perspective of these possibilities in an additional chapter. The difficulty here, like the entire topic of technology, is that dramatic shifts as new options occur almost daily. Nonetheless, we still have to endeavor to cover the basics especially because some people haven't had the opportunities to explore all areas or to look at the topic in its entirety.

This chapter begins with an overview of Web 2.0. We then look at the use of Web 2.0 tools as a resource and as a communication tool. Finally, we look at many different types of tools, such as blogs, wikis, online office applications, content sharing, and social networking.

WHAT IS WEB 2.0

Web 2.0 implies that it is the second version (or, more correctly speaking, second generation) of the Web. The first generation can be seen as one way communication. In that model, Webmasters created Web pages, placed content on those pages, and people would go to the sites to read that content. Content in this sense could have included images, video, and audio as well. Web pages were structured with html, and it took very specific and knowledgeable skills in order to make this possible, hence, the implication that one had to "master" this complex structure. Nonetheless, it still empowered more people than ever before to create and share their knowledge with others around the world. It was revolutionary.

The second generation, however, can be summarized as two-way communication. Many of these Web 2.0 tools involve the ability of or even expectation that others will view the site and add their own information, contributing to the creation of more content. In a sense, everyone becomes the author of that information. This is done through intuitive display layouts, websites that include all of the creation and editing features built in (although some sites may require some type of installation). This is also sometimes referred to as the social Web.

RESOURCES AND COMMUNICATION

Most of these Web 2.0 tools have a double-sided nature. The first is as a means for the teacher to provide information or content to students, parents, other teachers, or anyone else they wish. In the earlier days of the Web, it took a great deal of special knowledge, skills, and installed programs to create a website. With the intuitive and simpler interfaces and online access, this is no longer the case. This also means that there is often less flexibility and limitations with less options; the trade off is usually not a problem for most people. Rarely do you find that this is a limitation that needs to be overcome.

The other side of Web 2.0 tools is as a form of communication and collaboration. In this sense, students and others have the ability to share their ideas and information with each other and/or the teacher. Again, students will find simple interfaces and short learning curves. The ease of fast communication opens many different learning opportunities.

The following sections look closer at some of the major types of Web 2.0 tools. Although not a comprehensive list, it does provide an overview of the most common general categories.

BLOGS

A blog is a narrative in which the author can share information with others. It is presented in reverse chronological order, with the most recent post viewed at the top, pushing the older posts down the page toward the bottom. This allows immediate access to the most current information followed by some scrolling to get to the older posts. Largely textual like a form of a personal journal in nature, it can also include other media, such as images, video, or audio.

Blogs can be used by students in multiple ways, usually for some type of writing, reflecting, sharing lesson. Students can use blogs to track their thoughts and processes as they work on an assignment, submit written assignments to their teachers, share information with classmates in the same school or with others, or even write reviews for library books. Teachers can also use blogs to share content or information with their students or in place of parent newsletters.

Technical aspects of blogs need to be discussed at the school and district level. While teachers can always blog from home and share that with students and parents, when done from within school walls, issues of safety and filters comes into play. Questions about whether to use hosted services, free or fee-based hosts, or installing software on school servers need to be answered.

WIKIS

Wikis are Web pages that can be edited without having to download or install Web editing software. Depending on the individual wiki, they may be open to editing by anyone, those with accounts from that wiki, or those specifically invited to edit. The *Wikipedia* is probably one of the most well known and largest of wikis.

Wikis can be utilized by students as a way to share information, but the greatest benefit is when they are used collaboratively. By allowing students to work on a single Web page and add and change information, students are able to easily complete assignments in a social atmosphere instead of in isolation. Teachers are also excited about wikis as an easy way to share information with students and parents without having to worry about complex Web-editing software or having to upload files to a Web server. This then becomes a way to replace classroom Web pages.

Technical aspects here also touch on safety and access. Although schools can host their own wikis on their servers, this Web 2.0 tool is most often hosted off campus from a variety of vendors. Therefore, school filters must be adjusted to allow this access.

ONLINE OFFICE APPLICATIONS

Online office applications are Web versions of office suites, allowing users to use word-processing, spreadsheet, and presentation tools without having to download or install software. Although these applications are sometimes criticized for having fewer features and being less robust than complete suites like Microsoft Office, that simplicity actually makes it easier for students to use with very short learning curves. Additionally, most users only use a small percentage of features from office suites, so online suites end up meeting the needs of most students.

Online office applications can be utilized by students similar to wikis, as a way to complete assignments, submit work, and work collaboratively with other classmates. The advantage to these suites is in the presentation aspects, number crunching of spreadsheets, and the look and feel of word processing for their work.

Teachers and students alike can enjoy the ability to create presentations and share them with others without having to worry about what software is installed. Anyone with Internet access will be able to create, view, and use these tools at no cost.

CONTENT SHARING

Content sharing sites are websites where you can store resources for future use. This can include the actual content itself or simply links to those resources. They can be for your own use or to share with others.

Examples of content sharing sites include *YouTube* and *TeacherTube*. As a collection of videos, teachers might want to upload their own content so that their students have access for future lessons, or you could use the wealth of resources already there from other people. Sites like *Delicious* are useful as a way to store links to websites that you'll want to visit again in the future, basically storing bookmarks on the Web, as opposed to tied to a single computer.

As with all of these sites, conversations with technology coordinators is important to ensure that access is not blocked within the schools. If so, there are sometimes ways around them. For instance, some teachers will find *YouTube* videos at home, download the video to a flash drive, and then bring it to school the next day to play. *Mydownloadvideo* is one such site that makes this an easy process.

SOCIAL NETWORKING

Social networking sites allow communities of students to work together, share information and resources, and communicate in a social environment. Although the social aspect is most widely used, these sites are powerful tools that mimic course-management systems. In the higher-education setting, faculty do not have the same concerns for safety, but in K–12 schools it is not appropriate to use *Facebook* or *MySpace* with students. However, some safer environments, such as *Ning*, allow private communities to be set up, ensuring that outsiders do not have access to students.

These social networking sites mimic the functionality of many course-management systems. They include the ability to communicate via discussions, upload and share documents, incorporate audio and video in addition to text, share links and resources, and (for teachers) an easy way to post announcements.

WEBSITES

Blogger: www.blogger.com
Delicious: http://delicious.com
ePals: http://sites.epals.com
Google Docs: http://docs.google.com
Mydownloadvideo: www.mydownloadvideo.com
Ning: www.ning.com
PBworks: http://pbworks.com
TeacherTube: www.teachertube.com
Wikipedia: www.wikipedia.org
Wikispaces: www.wikispaces.com
WordPress : http://wordpress.org
YouTube: www.youtube.com
Zoho: www.zoho.com

Bibiliography

American Association of School Librarians. *Standards for the 21ˢᵗ Century Learner*. Chicago: American Library Association, 2007.

American Association of School Librarians and Association for Educational Communications and Technology. *Information Power: Building Partnerships for Learning*. Chicago: American Library Association, 1998.

———. *Information Power: Guidelines for School Library Media Programs*. Chicago: American Library Association, 1988.

American Library Association and National Education Association. *Standards for School Media Programs*. Chicago: American Library Association, 1969.

Anderson, Mary A. "Creating Tech-Savvy Teachers." *School Library Journal* 49, no. 2 (February 2003): 6–7.

Auger, Brian. "Living with Linux." *Library Journal Net Connect* (Spring 2004): 16–18.

Babcock, Charles. "HP Upgrades Thin Clients in Wake of Windows 7." *InformationWeek*. 2009. www.informationweek.com/news/software/hosted/showArticle.jhtml?articleID=222000355 (accessed December 2, 2009).

Baker, Andrea, and Amy Daniels. "Chicks in Charge." *Library Journal* 129, no. 5 (March 15, 2004): 46.

Baran, Paul. "On Distributed Communications Networks." *IEEE Transactions on Communications Systems* CS-12, no. 1 (March 1964): 1–9.

Barton, Miriam. "Getting Wired: A School Computer Network." *LLA Bulletin* 61, no. 3 (Winter 1999): 184–87.

Bennett, Harvey. "Successful K–12 Technology Planning: Ten Essential Elements." *Teacher Librarian* 31, no. 1 (October 2003): 22–25.

Benson, Allen C. *Neal-Schuman Complete Internet Companion for Librarians.* New York: Neal-Schuman, 2001.

Bilal, Dania. *Automating Media Centers and Small Libraries.* Greenwood Village, CO: Libraries Unlimited, 2002.

Bodine, Cathy. "Assistive Technology and the Educational Process." *Colorado Libraries* 28, no. 4 (2002): 28–30.

Boeri, Robert J. "Office 2003 InfoPath and MS Word Professional." *EContent* 26, no. 11 (November 2003): 17–19.

Boettiger, Adam. "Tips and Techniques with Windows XP." *Nebraska Library Association Quarterly* 34, no. 2 (Summer 2003): 22–27.

Brandt, D. S. "Create Your Own 'Quick-and-Dirty' Handouts." *Computers in Libraries* 22, no. 2 (February 2002): 39–41.

Braun, Linda. "In Virtual Pursuit." *School Library Journal Net Connect* (Fall 2001): 32–34.

Breeding, Marshall. "A Hard Look at Wireless Networks." *Library Journal Net Connect* (Summer 2002): 14–17.

Butler, Rebecca P. "Workshop Handouts—Can I Share Them with My Colleagues?" *Knowledge Quest* 33, no. 2 (November/December 2004): 71–72.

Caro, Diane. "School Library Web Site: This Virtual Library Is Always Open." *Colorado Libraries* 27, no. 3 (2001): 7–8.

Cheswick, William, Steven Bellovin, and Aviel Rubin. *Firewalls and Internet Security: Repelling the Wily Hacker.* Boston: Addison-Wesley, 2003.

Clyde, Anne. "Creating the School Library Web Site." *Teacher Librarian* 29, no. 3 (2002): 25–28.

———. "School Library Web Sites." *Teacher Librarian* 28, no. 2 (2000): 51–53.

Cohn, John M., Ann L. Kelsey, and Keith Michael Fiels. *Writing and Updating Technology Plans.* New York: Neal-Schuman, 1999.

Collins Dictionary of Computing (2000). "Email or e-mail." www.xreferplus.com/entry/1252851 (accessed October 19, 2004).

———. "Internet." www.xreferplus.com/entry/1253681 (accessed October 19, 2004).

———. "WWW (World Wide Web)." www.xreferplus.com/entry/1256208 (accessed October 19, 2004).

Curry, Ann, and Ken Haycock. "Filtered or Unfiltered?" *School Library Journal* 47, no 1. (January 2001): 43–47.

Davies, Joseph. *Deploying Secure 802.11 Wireless Networks with Microsoft Windows.* Redmond, WA: Microsoft, 2004.

Edwards, Julie-Ann, Mike Hartnell, and Rosalind Martin. "Interactive Whiteboards: Some Lessons from the Classroom." *Micromath* 18, no. 2 (2002): 30.

Fennelly, Lawrence J. *Handbook of Loss Prevention and Crime Prevention.* Boston: Butterworth-Heinemann, 1996.

Fryer, Wesley A. "Working with Reluctant Teachers." *Technology & Learning* 25, no. 11 (June 2005): 12.

Gardner, Howard. *Frames of Mind: The Theory of Multiple Intelligences.* New York: Basic Books, 1993.

Geisert, Paul G., and Mynga K. Futrell. *Teachers, Computers, and Curriculum: Microcomputers in the Classroom.* Needham Heights, MA: Pearson Education, 2000.

Gordon, Ross. "Thin Client Architecture in Libraries." *Feliciter* 47, no. 2 (2001): 78–80.

Grignano, Domenic. "12 Tips for Launching a Wireless Laptop Program." *Technology & Learning* 25, no. 3 (2004): 37–40.

Hannon, Scott M. "Building a Better Staff." *School Library Journal* 49, no. 2 (February 2003): 4–5.

Held, Gilbert. *Ethernet Networks: Design, Implementation, Operation, Management.* New York: Wiley, 1998.

Henry J. Kaiser Family Foundation, *See No Evil: How Internet Filters Affect the Search for Online Health Information,* www.kff.org/entmedia/20021210a-index.cfm (accessed April 15, 2005).

Huber, Joe. "Buzzing about New Technologies." *Book Report* 20, no. 4 (January/February 2002): 50.

———. "Desktop Security . . . Now More Than Ever." *Library Media Connection* 23, no. 4 (January 2005): 58.

"It All Started with Babbage." *Computerworld* 39, no. 31 (August 1, 2005): 28.

Jurkowski, Odin. "Schools of Thought: What to Include on Your School Library Web Site." *Children & Libraries: The Journal of the Association for Library Service to Children* 3, no. 1 (2005): 24–28.

Kienzle, Claudia. "Mac Aficionado Turned PC Enthusiast." *EMedia* 16, no. 4 (April 2003 supplement): S9.

Kilgour, Frederick G. *The Evolution of the Book.* New York: Oxford University Press, 1998.

Knox, Helen. "How Are We Doing? A Security System in a School Library." *The School Librarian* 42 (November 1994): 142–43.

Kochtanek, Thomas R., and Joseph R. Matthews. *Library Information Systems: From Library Automation to Distributed Information Access Solutions.* Westport, CT: Libraries Unlimited, 2002.

Koss, Linda. "Filtering Is Not the Answer." *Library Journal* 130, no. 1 (January 2005): 70.

Kranich, Nancy. "Why Filters Won't Protect Children or Adults." *Library Administration & Management* 18, no. 1 (Winter 2004): 14–18.

Latham, Joyce. "Everything Old Is Thin Again." *School Library Journal Net Connect* (Fall 2001): 20–22.

Lester, June, and Kathy H. Latrobe. "The Education of School Librarians." In *The Emerging School Library Media Center: Historical Issues and Perspectives*, edited by Kathy H. Latrobe, 1–15. Englewood, CO: Libraries Unlimited, 1998.

Mackall, Phil. "Interactive Whiteboards Enhance the Learning Experience for Deaf, Hard-of-Hearing Students." *T.H.E. Journal* 31, no. 10 (2004): 64–66.

March, Tom, "The Learning Power of WebQuests." *Educational Leadership* 61, no. 4 (December 2003): 42–46.

Mather, Becky. *Creating a Local Area Network in the School Library Media Center*. Westport, CT: Greenwood, 1997.

Matthews, Joseph R. *Technology Planning: Preparing and Updating a Library Technology Plan*. Westport, CT: Libraries Unlimited, 2004.

Maxymuk, John, *Using Desktop Publishing to Create Newsletters, Handouts, and Web Pages: A How-to-Do It Manual*. New York: Neal-Schuman, 1997.

Minkel, Walter. "A Filter That Lets Good Information In." *School Library Journal* 50, no. 3 (March 2004): 28–30.

———. "Gotcha!" *School Library Journal* 48, no. 10 (October 2002), 54–55.

———. "It's Not Rocket Science: Making Your Site's List of Links Supremely Useful Isn't All That Difficult." *School Library Journal* 48, no. 6 (2002): 31.

———. "Linux at the Right Price." *School Library Journal* 49, no. 4 (April 2003): 32–33.

———. "A Smarter System." *School Library Journal* 49, no. 11 (November 2003): 48–51.

———. "Stretch Your Network." *School Library Journal* 48, no. 8 (August 2002): 52–53.

———. "We're Not Just a Building." *Library Journal Net Connect* (Spring 2003): 26–27.

———. "Who's Blocking Whom? School Librarians Have Little Say in Online Filtering Decisions." *School Library Journal* 49, no. 6 (June 2003): 35.

Missouri Department of Elementary and Secondary Education. *School Library Media Standards Handbook*. 2003. http://dese.mo.gov/divimprove/ curriculum/library (accessed June 3, 2006).

———. *Show-Me Connection: An Additional Study on the Relationship between School Library Media Services and Student Achievement*. http://dese.mo.gov/ divimprove/curriculum/librarystudy/libraryresearch2.pdf (accessed June 22, 2004).

———. *Standards for Missouri School Library Media Centers*. 2002. http://dese .mo.gov/divimprove/curriculum/standards/02standards.pdf (accessed June 3, 2006).

Morgan, Candace. "Internet Filtering and Individual Choice." *Oregon Library Association Quarterly* 10, no. 4 (Winter 2004): 5–7.

Morris, Betty J. *Administering the School Library Media Center.* Westport, CT: Libraries Unlimited, 2004.

Moschovitis, Christos J. P., Hilary Poole, Tami Schuyler, and Theresa M. Senft. *History of the Internet.* Santa Barbara, CA: ABC-CLIO, 1999.

Ozer, Jan. "The Power and Influence of Photoshop." *EMedia* 16, no. 10 (October 2003): 56.

Pace, Andrew. "E-books: Round Two." *American Libraries* 35, no. 8 (2004): 74–75.

Papert, Seymour. *The Children's Machine: Rethinking School in the Age of the Computer.* New York: Basic Books, 1993.

Piaget, Jean. *The Essential Piaget.* Edited by Howard E. Gruber and J. Jacques Vonèche. New York: Basic Books, 1977.

Peek, Robin. "The Battle of the Windows." *Information Today* 21, no. 2 (February 2004): 15–16.

Peters, Kathleen A. "Drowning in PC Management: Could a Linux Solution Save Us?" *Information Today* 24, no. 6 (June 2004): 6–8, 60–64.

Reardon, Tom. "Interactive Whiteboards in School: Effective Uses." *Media & Methods* 38, no. 7 (2002): 12.

Rensberger, Dave. "Fast Track and Free: OpenOffice 1.0." *Searcher* 11, no. 5 (May 2003): 46–48.

Roberts, Linda. "Harnessing Information Technology for International Education." *Phi Delta Kappan* 86, no. 3 (November 2004): 225–28.

Roblyer, M. D. *Integrating Educational Technology into Teaching.* Upper Saddle River, NJ: Pearson Education, 2003.

Rockman, Saul. "A Study in Learning." *Technology & Learning* 25, no. 3 (2004): 34–40.

Saettler, Paul. *Evolution of American Educational Technology.* Englewood, CO: Libraries Unlimited, 1990.

Seels, Barbara B., and Rita C. Richey. *Instructional Technology: The Definition and Domains of the Field.* Washington, DC: Association for Educational Communications and Technology, 1994.

Sheehan, Mark. "Thin Clients and Network-Centric Computing." *Online* 22, no. 6 (November/December 1998): 89–92.

Shute, Valerie J., and Joseph Psotka. "Intelligent Tutoring Systems: Past, Present, and Future." In *Handbook of Research for Educational Communications and Technology,* edited by David H. Jonassen, pp. 570–600. New York: Macmillan, 1996.

Sikora, Axel. *Wireless Personal and Local Area Networks.* West Sussex, England: Wiley, 2003.

Slowinski, Joe. "What Will the Future of Education Look Like?" *Book Report* 20, no. 4 (January/February 2002): 18–20.

Speer, Susan, and Angelucci, Daniel. "Extending the Reach of the Thin Client." *Computers in Libraries* 21, no. 3 (March 2001): 46–50.

Tolppanen, Bradley. "Electronic Detection Systems: Is Your Library Ready for One?" *Louisiana Libraries* 63, no. 2 (Fall 2000): 7–11.

Tolzman, Don H., Alfred Hessel, and Reuben Peiss. *The Memory of Mankind: The Stories of Libraries since the Dawn of History.* New Castle, DE: Oak Knoll Press, 2001.

U.S. Department of Education, National Center for Education Statistics. *The Status of Public and Private School Library Media Centers in the United States: 1999–2000*, NCES 2004-313. Edited by Barbara Holton, Yupin Bae, Susan Baldridge, Michelle Brown, and Dan Heffron. Washington, DC: U.S. Department of Education, 2004. http://nces.ed.gov/pubs2004/2004313.pdf (accessed June 3, 2006).

Vassos, Kristen. "Classroom Instruction with Electronic Whiteboards." *Media & Methods* 41, no. 2 (2004): 20–33.

Zacker, Craig. *Networking: The Complete Reference.* Berkeley, CA: McGraw-Hill, 2001.

Index

About the Author

Dr. Odin Jurkowski is associate professor at the University of Central Missouri (UCM), where he coordinates the Educational Technology Program and chairs the Department of Career and Technology Education. He's been at UCM since 2002, having completed his MLS from Dominican University, an MS in technical communications and information design from Illinois Institute of Technology, and his EdD in instructional technology from Northern Illinois University. He teaches Foundations of Educational Technology, Using Technology to Enhance Teaching and Learning, Communication in Online Learning Communities, Educational Technology Leadership, and in the past has also taught Integration and Utilization, Information Technology in Library Media Centers, Creating Web Based Resources, History of the Book and Libraries, and much more.

Dr. Jurkowski, like many educators, has always been a proponent and heavy user of libraries, from youthful days in the public library to school and academic libraries. His undergraduate internship in the Public Information Office at the American Library Association headquarters in Chicago prompted him to take his career in that direction. From librarian to head of a branch to library director, he later transitioned into university teaching after completing his doctorate.